AGILE BUSINESS

A Leader's Guide to Harnessing Complexity

By

Bob Gower

&

Rally Software

RALLY
SOFTWARE

AGILE BUSINESS — *A Leader's Guide to Harnessing Complexity*

Published by:
Rally Software Development Corp.
3333 Walnut Street
Boulder, Colorado 80301
www.rallydev.com

Permissions:
For permission information and authorization to photocopy items for corporate, personal or educational use, please contact:

Legal Department
Rally Software Development Corp.
3333 Walnut Street
Boulder, Colorado 80301

Author:
Bob Gower
www.bobgower.com

Book and e-book design:
Telemachus Press, LLC
www.telemachuspress.com

Cover design:
Grant Miller

ISBN: 978-1-939337-53-5 (print)
ISBN: 978-1-939337-52-8 (ebook)

Version 2013.05.02

Printed in the United State of America
10 9 8 7 6 5 4 3 2 1

Acclaim for *Agile Business*

"*Agile Business* is more than just a savvy guide to the ins and outs of the Agile Development process. It is a call to take your game up to a new level where customers are not only satisfied but delighted, and where work teams are not only productive but inspired."
Geoffrey Moore, author, *Crossing the Chasm*

"It's hard to be Lean if you're not Agile too. *Agile Business* is a powerful collection of essays by Agile thought leaders and practitioners. It will help you understand and apply Agile principles in the real world. Don't miss it!"
Patrick Vlaskovits, author, *The Entrepreneur's Guide to Customer Development*

"*Agile Business* describes Agile philosophy and practices in elegant and simple terms, making the concepts easy to grasp and, more importantly, easy to use. I've struggled for years to help my business partners understand how to work with Agile teams and how to best leverage Agile for themselves. This book provides a foundation to effectively use Agile to collaborate with partners across your entire organization. Thanks Rally!"
Geoffrey Bourne, SVP at a multinational financial services corporation

"Agile is one of the best ways I know to create happier and more democratic organizations. And this new book from Rally is the most accessible introduction to Agile I've ever seen. If you're new to the topic or want to deepen your practice, then *Agile Business* is the place to start."
Traci Fenton, founder and CEO, WorldBlu

"There are few Agile coaching communities as full of integrity, goodwill, self-reflection, learning, and improvement and application experience as Rally's. I have enjoyed my dance with Rally as a client, partner, collaborator, friend, and inspiration for nearly ten years. This book is a treasure trove of knowledge and a pleasure to read."
Christopher Avery, international speaker, author and business advisor

"Any sustainable business must meet customer needs with efficiency and flexibility. *Agile Business* describes how to do just that. The lessons here

aren't just for software companies. Any business creating complex products can benefit from Agile and Lean thinking. *Agile Business* is the way to learn."
L. Hunter Lovins, president and founder, Natural Capital Solutions

"The time is right for Agile to escape software delivery and transform the business—this book provides instructions on how to build your escape plan."
Dave West, chief product officer, Tasktop Technologies, and former Forrester Research analyst

"Agile is not just for software developers! The biggest mistake I see made by entrepreneurs and business people at all levels is planning too far ahead and then getting stuck in their plan. They stick to their original plan even when everything indicates it is time to abandon the plan, reassess the goals, and regroup. Learning the skills, tools, and methodology of Agile, however, will help you avoid making this common and costly mistake. If you're curious to learn exactly what Agile is—or how to organize incredibly complex projects around constantly shifting goals and resources—this book is your answer! And it's written in clear, nontechnical prose."
Rich Goldstein, founder, Goldstein Patent Law

"A great reference guide for businesses and individuals wanting to explore the many dimensions of being more Agile. Nicely broad, nicely topical."
Dean Leffingwell, author, *Agile Software Requirements* and *Scaling Software Agility*

"A powerful book that delivers years of knowledge and expertise in a relatable and captivating way."
Andrew Korbel, Agile Coach, DigitalGlobe

In loving memory of my father, Irv Gower (1925-2012), who always reminded me that inch by inch life's a cinch.

Contents

Acknowledgments

No book is the work of a single individual and this book—a collaboratively written book about collaboration—took a village. Many people contributed and often in more than one way.

First, I'd like to thank all of the contributing authors. This book is what it is because of your willingness to take time out of incredibly busy lives to share your experience and wisdom. You are 35 of the most caring and brilliant people I know. Thank you, Alex Pukinskis, Andre Dhondt, Ann Konkler, Ben Carey, Brendan Walsh, Brent Barton, Charles Ferenchack, Chris Browne, Eric Willeke, Isaac Montgomery, Jean Tabaka, Jeff Ellis, Jessica Kahn, Jim Tremlett, John Michael Martin, Julie Byrne, Julie Chickering, Karl Scotland, Ken Clyne, Larry Maccherone, Laura Burke, Liz Andora, Mark Kilby, Michael Ball Marian, Niki Kohari, Rachel Weston Rowell, Rick Simmons, Ronica Roth, Ryan Martens, Sean Heuer, Stephanie Tanner, Steve Lawrence, Tamara Nation, Todd Olson, and Zach Nies.

A writer is nothing without a good editorial team. Thank you to our editor and publishing advisor, Michael Parrish DuDell, who took us from hope to strategy to finished product; and to copyeditor Richard Defendorf, whose attention to detail is unparalleled. And a special thank you to Kevin Kanarek—a dear friend who has been honing my writing and storytelling for many years and who offered keen insight into early drafts of this book.

Steve Jackson and the team at Telemachus Press, thank you for giving us such a beautiful layout and helping us navigate the treacherous waters of digital formats. And thank you to Grant Miller for the wonderful cover design.

This book has been through many incarnations at Rally and work on early versions with Scott Dunn, Steve Adolph, and Isaac Montgomery was an invaluable step toward the finished product we have today.

Producing a book at a software company is a bit like building a bicycle in a machine shop. All the parts are there but you're not really set up to do the work in an easy or efficient way. This book wouldn't have happened without the early and continuous support of Ryan Martens, Tim Miller, and Jean Tabaka—thank you for your time and attention. And thank you to Anne Greenhaw, Bob Nendza, Brad Norris, Chris James, Christine Bottagaro, Jessica Kahn, Kerri Beers, Lara Vacante, Nick Budor, Parker Jackson, Rachel Weston Rowell, Ronica Roth, and Zach Nies for contributing time, resources, and encouragement at numerous points throughout the project.

Many outside advisors influenced this book. Special thanks go to Alan Weiss, Andrew Korbel, Ben Buxton, Brad Feld, Chad Holdorf, Chris Coffin, Craig Fischberg, Heather Kanser, Israel Gat, Josh Cha, Josh Gampp, Kimon Papahadjopoulos, Laureen Knudsen, Linda Ziemke, Matt Blumberg, Matt Weir, Peter Lavoie, Tim Martindale, and Troy Bailey.

For help navigating the complex world of writing and publishing a first book, I owe a huge debt of gratitude to Alexandra Jamieson (who famously asked, "Do you have an outline?"), Alicia Dunams, Beth Barany, Jonathan Fields, Michael Ellsberg, and Michael Parrish DuDell.

My early understanding of systems thinking, lean manufacturing, and Agile was guided by an incredible group of people. Special thanks go to Aaron Sanders, Alexander and Kathia Laszlo, Alex Wong, Bob Dunham, Brian Burt, Chris Conser, Eric Babinet, Hunter Lovins, John Cook, Jørgen Vos, Lisa Abbott, Marcy Swenson, Richard Calosso, Tom Looy, and William Pietri for your help and companionship on my journey.

And to friends new and old who guide and advise me on a daily basis, thank you Adam Griffiths, Asil Toskal, Beth Crittenden, Bryan Franklin, Dave Meader, Edward Loh, Eric Neuner, Eric Rude, Gregg Farrauto, Laura

Garnett, Mark Brenwall, Mark McMillan, Meghna Majmudar, Peter Shallard, Richard Goldstein, Susan Lee, Wolfram Arnold, and Yevgeniy Galper.

And finally, I am blessed with family who support me through thick and thin, simplicity and complexity, success and, well, let's call them *learning experiences*. Thank you to my partner in life, Alexandra Jamieson, whose patience, support and wisdom have seen me through many challenges; to my father, Irv Gower, who passed away before seeing this book completed but provided the wisdom and support essential to making it possible; and to my brother, George Gower, and mother, Nancy Gower, whose encouragement and support mean the world to me.

Thank you all. This book is yours.

Foreword

by Brad Feld

I've been a believer in Rally Software and its mission to create more Agile and sustainable companies since the very start. Ryan Martens launched the company just over 10 years ago in my office, and over the years I've watched it grow with great interest. At the time, Agile was confined to startups and small operations and was seen mostly as "that thing developers do." Over the past decade, however, Agile's influence has grown and, likewise, so has Rally's.

I'm an investor by trade and that means that I'm passionate about helping the companies I invest in, and advise, achieve profitability. This race to fit product to market and keep it there is what good companies do. And Agile is, I've found, an essential tool for any size company in today's complex markets.

Rally Software lives and breathes Agile and I can think of no company better suited to write the book that finally makes this complex and confusing topic accessible to the average business reader. Bob Gower has written a great book that will orient you to Agile and help you see for yourself how to begin applying it to your organization or deepen your practice if you're already on the path.

The book was collaboratively written and includes contributions from more than 30 people who are out in the field every day helping other companies adopt Agile principles. They see how Agile is practiced in the real world and have shared those stories and experiences here with you.

As Agile becomes more widespread in software, engineering in general, and all aspects of business, I'm honored to be involved with one of the companies that started the Agile movement. But Rally isn't stopping here. Ryan Martens recently spoke to Engineers Without Borders about using Agile methods to help combat global warming.

Rally has done amazing things in its first 10 years of existence; I look forward to the next decade of Rally and Agile!

Brad Feld
Foundry Group managing director, co-author of *Startup Life: Surviving and Thriving in a Relationship with an Entrepreneur.*
Boulder, Colorado, January 2013

A Message from the Founder

By Ryan Martens

Given the great Agile coaching professionals who work at Rally, writing a book has always been on our mind. However, in the past we thought it too difficult to publish a quality book while also delivering the many products and services that our fantastic customers have come to expect. That is until this year when we finally broke through. Thanks to increased scale, a reorganization of services, a dedicated leader, and a lean startup approach, we're excited to present *Agile Business*—our contribution to the Agile community.

vii

They say a picture is worth a thousand words, and I believe this graphic by Kathy Sierra beautifully sums up the mission behind our book.

Since I first saw this graphic, my goal has been to keep Rally and our customers on the Expert curve of Agile. What you will find in these pages is an extension of that goal: a series of short articles on strategy, process, people, and tools.

The job of servant leader and coach is to find ways to keep moving the organization forward. After 25 years in the software and systems industry, and 10 years working on Rally, I've come to believe that Agile and Lean concepts can do just that. Whether you're new to Agile or already an expert, I'm confident that this book will empower you with ideas and knowledge, and inspire you to seize the opportunity for you and your organization.

At Rally we very much value discussion, and I'd like to personally invite you to share your feedback about the book with us at rallydev.com/agilebook. If you'd like to learn more about our company or products and services, please feel free to contact me directly at ryan@rallysoftware.com.

Here is everything we know about staying on the Expert curve! We hope it brings value and prosperity to your organization.

Ryan Martens, CTO & Founder, @RallyOn (twitter)

Preface

In 2008, I was hired as the product manager at a new startup in Silicon Valley. The CEO and I decided it would be a good idea to try this thing called "Agile." Like everyone else, we wanted our product out the door faster, cheaper, and better, and Agile seemed like our best bet. It took us six months and quite a bit of struggle and confusion to get our system working well, and two more months to get the first version of the product out the door. But eventually, we looked back and realized we'd not only created a product that delighted our customers, but also a development methodology that delighted our team.

Agility took us from a group that argued and struggled to a team that collaborated and produced. It didn't eliminate our troubles, of course, but it made such a difference in our output and in our daily lives that I became a believer. I resolved to write a book that would help people like me, with more focus on the business than the technology, understand Agile and apply the principles in their—your—organization.

It's taken well over three years to get this book into print, and it's been a long and complex journey. I stopped and started the project several times, and the project shifted yet again in 2010 when I joined Rally Software and found myself surrounded by an incredible group of people who had insights and stories to share from their own circuitous journeys. I knew the book would be that much stronger if I included their voices and stories as well. I have not been disappointed.

Our goal with this book is to share our experience and knowledge in a language that can be easily grasped and put to use whether or not you have Agile—or even technology—experience.

An important part of Agile is working collaboratively, incrementally, and iteratively. We've done all three. This book has been a team effort and has been through several rounds of market feedback. This is our effort of practicing what we preach.

From everyone at Rally, we sincerely hope you enjoy.

Bob Gower, bobgower.com

How to Use This Book

Agile is complex. It takes a whole systems perspective of your business and therefore defies simple, linear explanation. Our goal with this book is to provide a clear, plain-language introduction to this topic.

In order to present the ideas as clearly as possible, we've divided the book into five simple parts:

1. **Build the Right Thing**, which covers product management, innovation, and product roadmaps.

2. **Build the Thing Right**, which covers the testing and engineering practices that contribute to organizational Agility.

3. **People, Not Resources**, which focuses on management practices and organizational culture building that motivate individuals to do great work.

4. **Agile Steering**, which covers dynamic planning and funding models that are compatible with a more Agile way of operating.

5. **Transform Your Organization**, which lays out the path for getting from where you are now to where you want to be as an organization.

Each of the 60 essays in *Agile Business* is designed to stand alone. We've avoided jargon and defined new terms wherever they appear. The book can be read cover to cover, of course, or you can pick and choose only the pieces that interest you.

If you'd like a quick overview, we recommend reading the introduction to the book, followed by the introductory essays for each section. This will give you a sound foundation. From there you can dive into the individual topics that interest you.

And if at any point you feel ready to take some action, then jump to the *Your Next Steps* section at the end of the book.

AGILE BUSINESS

Introduction

By Bob Gower

Gall's Law: A complex system that works is invariably found to have evolved from a simple system that worked. A complex system designed from scratch never works and cannot be patched up to make it work. You have to start over with a working simple system.

—John Gall

At the beginning of a new coaching relationship, I always start with a conversation about the business goals the customer is aiming for. And I almost always hear some combination of the same few items: better products, less waste, more predictability, happier people, and a shorter time to market. If you're reading this book it's likely you're looking for one or more of these things yourself.

I could easily end the conversation with these business goals and get started—Agile development practices, after all, have been demonstrably improving these metrics for more than 10 years. But when I let the conversation go a layer deeper, into more personal aspirations, I find what we all really want is a workplace that works—we want to enjoy our time at work while creating sustained value for our customers and ourselves.

How we create these kinds of organizations is the question that keeps me up at night, and not just for academic reasons. This way of working is not only good business, it's good global citizenship. Companies that inspire and empower their people to succeed are of vital importance. Rally strives to be one of those companies, and it's our mission to help others on the path: to build organizations that do well and do good. The Rally Mission states, "We believe empowered people who actually want to come to work are essential for solving today's big, complex problems."

This means we must take the Agile mindset out of a strictly development context and look at businesses as whole systems that are designed to solve problems and provide value. This is what we mean by Agile Business. And whether you're out to solve a tough problem for all of humanity, create an innovative product for a market niche, or extend the value of a complex system already in production, we invite you to join us on this path.

Vicious to Virtuous
If we are to transform our organizations, we must find a way to turn the wasteful, vicious cycles that derail us into virtuous cycles that create value.

When I was a child in Philadelphia in the 1970s, there was a lot of worry about the cycle of urban decay. Throughout my years in the professional world, I've seen similar worry about the kind of decay that destroys an organization. In software organizations, a common vicious cycle may look something like this: buggy technology leads to unhappy customers, which leads to unhappy managers who then pressure workers, who become unhappy and disengaged only to produce more buggy software.

It's likely that you're aware of cycles like this in your own organization, and you're looking for something that will help solve the problem. Sound about right? But the challenge with cycles is that they are not only cyclical and self-reinforcing, they are also complex. Is it poverty that feeds crime or crime that feeds poverty? Is it unhappy employees who make buggy code or buggy code that creates unhappy employees?

If we're to tackle these cycles in our lives and businesses, we need to be smart about where and how we intervene. And we must be conscious of the butterfly effect: small changes can have a huge impact for good or ill. The trick is to know where to start and how fast to move.

Agile is whole-system way of looking at, and acting on, your business. We work on the habits, individual attitudes, and organizational structures that support business as usual, and then we interrupt those patterns and build better organizations and products.

Healthy Systems

Agile, because it has a whole-system focus, is complex and can be challenging to understand. To simplify things a bit, we've organized this book into five sections. Each section is a view of a different facet of the same overarching topic and set of ideas. Taken together, they give a fairly complete picture of a healthy complex system—a business, your business.

Build the Right Thing: When I worked in newspapers we used to joke that "we don't have time to write it short," the observation being that concise writing takes more effort than verbose writing. The same is true of the development of any complex and innovative product. Great companies build products that customers love. While this means they build valuable and useful features, it also means they don't build things that aren't valuable.

Really great software is created by organizations that manage to put the customer at the center of their thinking and then work iteratively and incrementally to offer and test products to see what delights and what doesn't.

The Agile principles that help Build the Right Thing are: incremental delivery of value, team empathy for the customer, rapid prototyping, the Product Owner, and dynamic steering at the portfolio level.

Build the Thing Right: Every business wants products that scale well, perform as expected, and contain no unpleasant surprises for customers— or for future developers who must add new functionality. And this means we need to coordinate the efforts of a lot of smart, opinionated people. A shift to Agile engineering is more about a shift in mindset than it is about any specific practice or technology.

Toyota revolutionized quality in car manufacturing by empowering each employee to stop the line if a defect was spotted—something previously unheard of and unimaginable. It also created systems that made employees accountable to each other, not just to management. Agile leverages this same mindset by creating cross-functional teams that include members from both business and technology. The team members collectively agree on what "quality" means in their organization. Once the decision has been made, the team coordinates to ensure that these standards are maintained.

Agile principles that help Build the Thing Right are: team empathy for end user, requirements discovery and elaboration methodologies like Scrum or Kanban, local planning—those who do the work, plan the work—and team autonomy to "pull" work at their own pace and coordinate with other teams.

People, Not Resources: Henry Ford once lamented, "Why is it every time I ask for a pair of hands, they come with a brain attached?" With the creativity that's required from workers today, we don't have the luxury of trying to reduce people to a pair of hands. We not only want a brain, but one that is actively engaged and making the smartest decisions possible.

The goal of any management system or organizational design is to align people and get them pulling in the same direction. If people are pulling in different directions—as they are in many organizations—then a lot of effort can be expended with very little forward motion. In many organizations it's even common for people to actively work against each other. With Agile we work to create systems that allow people to feel aligned in ways that work for actual humans.

Agile principles that help treat people as People, not Resources, are: collaboration, servant leadership, self-organization and management, individual control of the work environment, and organizational transparency.

Agile Steering: Markets are dynamic, customers are fickle, and learning is a fluid process. This means that great organizations must have practices in place that allow them to frequently change direction and respond to new information and conditions.

Agile planning practices are both disciplined and dynamic. We allow for a freer flow of information, which means we can steer our organization like a bicycle, continually making subtle or not-so-subtle shifts in direction to respond to the current situation. And because we work in small increments of value, we are also able to deliver a steady stream of value to customers.

Agile principles that help with Agile Steering are: a steady cadence of planning, multi-level planning practices, transparency, retrospectives, information radiation, and staged funding.

Transform Your Organization: While all of these characteristics may sound like wonderful things to have in our companies, they are useless if we don't have a map or path for getting there from where we are now. Many organizations start a transformation to a new way of doing things only to drop out or, worse, get stuck in mediocrity.

At Rally, we've come to value an incremental and Agile approach to organizational change. We focus first on learning—by actually launching a few teams—then crafting larger experiments that set us up to deepen our Agile practice and expand it to other projects. Ultimately our goal is to develop learning organizations that get continually better.

Agile principles that help Transform Your Organization are: value-focused metrics, emphasizing vision and culture, continuous improvement, facilitation, coaching, and learning-focused processes.

It's the System

When we look around our businesses and see room for improvement, it's tempting to want to shake things up or change personnel. But if you look closer, you'll notice that the trouble is not the individuals but the system. Change the system and you'll change the behavior.

This is not to say that there won't be personnel changes along the way. It's likely that you may need to shift a few positions or let some people go. Often people who are not suited for the new way of doing things will self-select out. The transparency and steady production pace of an Agile workplace is difficult for those who like to hide out or simply coast.

In the 1980s, General Motors (GM) and Toyota entered into a joint venture at the New United Motor Manufacturing, Inc. (NUMMI) plant in Fremont, California. In a few short years, they turned one of the worst facilities in the industry—in terms of union complaints, product quality, and financial performance—into one of the most productive.

And they did it with the same people.

The union leadership that presided over a plant where drugs, alcohol, and sex were available for purchase (and that many likened to a prison) was the same group of people who built a system that transformed both performance and the lives of the workers. In fact, many workers reported that working at NUMMI gave meaning to their lives.

Your organization may not be in such dire straits, but you wouldn't be reading this book unless you felt some change was needed. We've seen Agile revolutionize organizations of all shapes and sizes and are certain that positive transformation is available for you, if you're ready and willing to make the necessary changes.

Thank you for picking up this book and starting the journey.

1

Build the Right Thing

Build the Right Thing

By Bob Gower

It doesn't matter how beautiful your theory is, it doesn't matter how smart you are. If it doesn't agree with experiment, it's wrong.

—Richard P. Feynman

Years ago when I worked in newspaper advertising, we would say that we knew half of our marketing efforts were working—just not which half. And when I became a software product manager, I found I was plagued by a similar uncertainty: I knew that our customers would use only about half of our features, but I had no idea which half.

If you're in charge of a software product, you probably stay up at night worried about which features to spend your time and budget on. From my position as a consultant working with various teams on numerous applications, I recognize that the development of unused features is the single biggest waste of time and resources in the software industry. And it's waste that has cascading effects that, if left unchecked, can bring a company to its knees.

Building the wrong thing not only wastes time and money, it demoralizes the creative, intelligent, and in-demand team members who are working on the products, thus making hiring and retention more difficult. Here's how this can happen:

Feature bloat, as we call it, ends up hiding the most useful features from customers in a forest of things they don't want. Customers get frustrated and call your support people—who cost you money—and overwhelm them with requests. Finally, this overload of features makes the development of new capabilities more challenging, which again frustrates developers. And on we go in a vicious cycle that ends with a competitor stealing your market share because their product is cheaper, leaner, more elegantly designed, and easier to use.

Apple, by contrast, has built the most valuable company on the planet by simplifying products, reducing features, and creating applications and devices that are lean and useful. The company has found a way to consistently build the right thing.

The same opportunity exists at your company. While your product may not be as sexy as an iPad, it can still be simple, elegant, and beautiful if you're willing to take the steps needed to put the customer, and the customer's needs, at the center of your organization. This is the goal of the Agile mindset: to remove waste by creating an organization that focuses on discovering customers' needs and meeting those needs quickly and affordably. This is why we're in business, after all: to provide value to our customers. And not just current customers—new customers in new markets as well.

Why, then, do our businesses so often lose their way?

The first step to creating a customer-centric organization is awareness that there is a problem. We need to realize that the way we've been doing things with large up-front design and requirements documents is part of the problem. But what next? How do we begin to reform our systems to be more customer-focused? While there are several things we can do, there are three that stand out above all others.

Start with Vision
Many products have plans but few have visions. We have endless lists of features and capabilities but no unifying vision that everyone is working

toward. A product vision is a high-level view of the value you want to provide and an understanding of whom you want to provide it to. It's really that simple—in fact, the simpler the better.

I challenge you to poll five of your employees or coworkers at random and ask them what the vision of your product is. If yours is like most businesses, you'll get five different answers—perhaps wildly different. This is why many organizations are lost in internal struggles when employees should be collaborating to delight customers. Once you have a unified vision, however, it's relatively easy to decide on specific features, prioritize them against each other, and begin pulling in the same direction.

When working on this book, we identified Agile Champions—people within companies who want to lead change in their organization—as the people we wanted to serve. The vision for this book was to create something they find so valuable that they'll be compelled to share it with everyone in their organization.

Through interviews and conversations with several active champions, we decided the most valuable thing we could provide would be a book that helps build understanding and consensus around Agile transformation. Only once we had the vision locked in, and a few hypotheses well articulated, did we talk about specific content for the book and develop a plan for creating it.

The vision came first.

In essence, you are creating the high-level metrics and values of your product—and the organization that makes it. Without an explicitly stated vision, you're shooting in the dark. You may think you have consensus, but like blind men touching an elephant, it's likely each person on your team has a radically different view of the thing you are creating.

Go slowly and get this part right.

Release Early and Often

Whether we release features iteratively or use a continuous flow and deployment, it's important that we design our human processes and technical infrastructure so work can be done in steady, small increments of value.

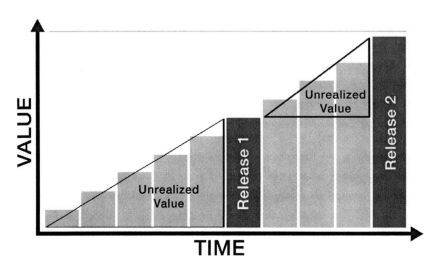

In this chart you can see the money that's left on the table when we insist on infrequent, big-bang releases. Incremental release means we're able to realize revenue early, but that's not its only benefit.

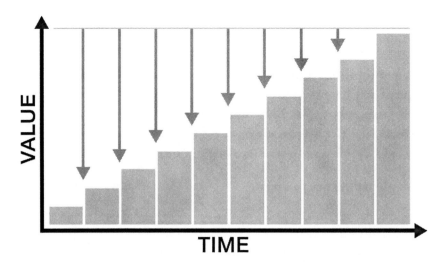

Incremental release means that we're able to observe early in the process how people are using our products and then incorporate what we learn into subsequent releases. This also means we experience a steady increase in what we know about our customers.

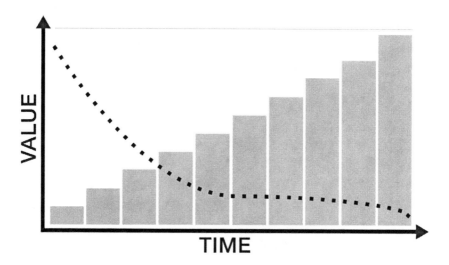

As our knowledge of the market increases, our risk goes down. Even if we are occasionally wrong, we can dynamically steer our product strategy, meaning even complete misses can have little impact on the bottom line and over time will become increasingly rare.

Work *with* Your Customer

Management guru Peter Drucker frequently pointed out that "doing the right thing is more important than doing things right." In order to do this we need to develop empathy; we must be able to sit in our customers' chair and see the world through their eyes.

Agile design practices encourage us to test our ideas quickly using tools like rapid prototyping, and to see our products in their natural habitat. Something as easy as hosting a weekly, catered lunch, during which your team watches customers actually use the product, can build team empathy and generate new ideas. I've never seen a team that does this enough.

Also, instituting the Product Owner role can have a far-reaching impact. A Product Owner is someone who sits on your development team and speaks for the customer, deciding what order features will be built in and whether or not a feature should actually be implemented—and if it is, what it needs to do in order to delight the customer. In some cases, a Product Owner can actually be a customer, but often this is just someone whose job it is to develop empathy and a keen sense of what's valuable. This *single wringable neck* between customer and developer provides the focus essential to building the right thing.

By creating a solid vision, shipping frequent releases, and engaging in an ongoing conversation with customers, you can begin to focus the collective attention of your organization on truly delighting your customer. While these few changes may seem relatively small, they will not only lead to better products but also to happier people and a healthier bottom line.

Agile and Innovation
By Ben Carey

A Foundation of Agility

So you've done the work to improve speed, quality, collaboration, and morale. You've got full, automated test coverage and have eliminated cycles lost to technical debt, bugs, and disagreement. But while you're confident you may be quickly building a high-quality product, one question still remains: are you sure you're building the *right* one?

While Agile has proven itself over the past 10 years to be an effective method for building products, this benefit often reveals a gap in many companies' processes. Once we improve how we build products, we often discover we must rethink the process behind how we decided to build the product in the first place. And it turns out Agile can help here, too.

As more organizations adopt Agile, new ideas are being developed to improve planning, roadmapping, and innovation. These pioneers are taking the process of building products to the next level through a deep understanding of the methods and principles of Agile.

Because Agile encourages information to flow both up and down the chain of command, it creates an opportunity to iterate not only the product, but the underlying definition of what exactly is being built. Establishing a set of Agile mental models gives us the foundation to explore new ways of approaching a host of activities—including innovation.

Models of Agile Innovation

Using common Agile ways of thinking, such as value-orientation, rapid iteration, and cross-functional teams, we begin to create an environment that is well-prepared for innovation. In many ways, Agile resembles the Design Thinking methods that have been pioneered in the last few decades, where diverse teams spend time developing empathy for the customer and then rapidly prototype possible solutions to iterate toward an ideal one.

If we have a foundation of Agile mental models during the development stage, then adding these more Agile practices to the specification isn't much of a leap at all. When Agile becomes more of a verb than a noun—when it becomes something we do rather than a defined process we apply—we know we're on the right track. And when we understand Agile to be a way of thinking and not a specific set of instructions, we have the capability to achieve higher degrees of impact.

An Alternative Posture for Building

The key to all of this is iteration. Iteration gives us a great delivery structure and approach for building, but it also helps us quickly discover alternatives for what and how we build.

Because we have the opportunity to see increments of our product in action, learn from user interaction, and apply that learning to what we're building, we not only get information about what works but also the opportunity to apply what we've learned to a change in direction and, perhaps, a new product.

Of course all this iteration only makes sense if our deliverables are value-focused. Because we are delivering discrete chunks of the most valuable things, we are continually testing our hypotheses about what the market will actually use. When trial is cheap and error is knowledge, we gain the ability to progress our solutions to the problems we are trying to solve—not just ship products out the door.

Using feedback in this way can open our eyes to horizons that we were unable to previously see. This is the heart of innovation. So our view of building begins to shift from simple incremental construction to a method of high-bandwidth learning, which can have dramatic impacts on the way we build software.

What all this means is that over time learning grows. We build better products and also gain a more sound understanding of the process behind how to build better products. The opportunity here is to develop organizations that are able to collaborate toward greatness and build beautiful businesses that create incredible products for grateful customers.

Sure, Agile can be approached as a means of reducing defects and costs and shortening time to market, but there is also an opportunity to iterate toward beauty, greatness, and impact. And we just happen to think that is` something worth working toward.

The Role of the Product Owner
By Sean Heuer

In most organizations, there is a gaping void between the team building the product and the customers using it. This gap is exacerbated when organizations create multiple layers of interfaces between the customer and the development team. What's more, this seems to be the rule, not the exception, in business today.

What this means is that there's no voice close to the development team that truly represents the needs of the customer—and the economics of the business—with the authority to set, or change, the direction of the product. Needless to say, this dramatically reduces the organization's ability to innovate, adapt, and deliver great products.

The Product Owner role is Agile's solution to this pervasive problem. Let's take a look at this unique position and examine the part it plays in a healthy product development cycle.

What is a Product Owner?
The Product Owner works with the development team on a daily, if not hourly, basis. Most Product Owners actually sit in the same room with developers. Their primary role is to connect the team with people outside the room: the customer, the business stakeholders, and sometimes other products and teams.

The Product Owner is responsible for managing the scope of the product or project and building empathy for the customer within the team. This means that he is responsible for delivering a product that meets the customer's needs. He also is responsible for answering team members' questions and helping them understand the customer's needs. Lastly, and possibly most important, he is responsible to the organization to make the best economic decisions.

While the Product Owner is the "single wringable neck" between the business and technology sides of the house, he is not there to prevent the team from contacting or interacting with the customer. In fact, great Product Owners encourage and enable frequent contact with the customer to build team empathy. However, they also know when it's time to stop conversation and start the action. This eliminates decisions by committee or, worse, inaction and indecision.

Successful Product Owners embody similar characteristics:

- They are great communicators.
- They have the ability to lead and motivate a group to pursue a vision, or they can take a back seat and listen with an open mind to customers and team members alike.
- They have domain knowledge in the areas being impacted by the product.
- They are decisive and courageous.
- They are collaborative while being capable negotiators.
- Lastly, and most important, they are trustworthy.

Story—The Extraordinary Product Owner
Over the years working with Agile teams, I have had the pleasure of knowing many great Product Owners. One Product Owner in particular—I call him the Extraordinary Product Owner—was particularly great at his job. He was paired with a somewhat dysfunctional team working on an unexciting accounting product. To make things worse, the project was under heavy scrutiny from every direction. Obviously, this was not the ideal

assignment for an up-and-comer. What he did with the opportunity, however, brought him recognition from the highest levels of the organization.

The first thing I noticed about the Extraordinary Product Owner was his enthusiasm and passion. This was apparent in his first presentation to the team, when he presented the vision for the product. I have seen many such presentations but his was the first I saw that tailored the message for the team and humanized the goal. He took the time to create more than a slide deck presenting the high-level scope and problem statement. He had video testimonials. He lined the walls with the personas of the key users. He did everything he could to put the team in the shoes of the customer. As it turned out, this presentation was only the beginning. He continued to work to bridge the gap between the team and the customer on a daily basis throughout the project.

The next thing I noticed was his ability to keep everyone in the loop. As I mentioned earlier, this project was under scrutiny from many stakeholders. If it weren't for the Extraordinary Product Owner's hard work to create, maintain, and frequently share easily understood visuals that displayed the progress of the work and the forecasted deliveries, the team may have drowned in systematic "help" from the stakeholders.

Another observation I had while watching the Extraordinary Product Owner was his ability to keep the team productive. He was able to balance the day-to-day work of answering team members' questions, clarifying customer needs, and making scoping decisions while staying four weeks ahead of the team in detailing out customer requirements. By maintaining a bucket of four weeks' worth of work for the team, he gave the team an opportunity to keep an eye on the future, balance dependencies between features, and maintain an even flow of features to the customer.

The last observation I had was the Extraordinary Product Owner's ability to negotiate with all parties to identify the best version of each feature, given the needs of the customer and the constraints of the project and technology. This included trusting the process to evolve each feature into its best form, while being decisive enough to maintain momentum.

Through the acts of the Extraordinary Product Owner, the team members delivered the product to the customer within the estimated timeline and under budget while earning the organization's highest customer satisfaction scores. This earned them a spot in the board of directors meeting, where they were greeted with applause and congratulations. Not bad for a gig nobody wanted.

There are many changes to the way teams approach the work in an Agile environment, and the Product Owner plays a key role in shaping that approach. To enable the transition to an Agile approach, you must invest in Product Owner competency that focuses on building empathy for the customer and managing product economics. Great code does not equal great products. Without empathy for our users and economics to drive decisions, all that great code may end up being wasted solving the wrong problem.

—

How to Staff Appropriately for a Successful Transition to Agile Product Management
(http://www.rallydev.com/agileblog/2012/09/how-to-staff-appropriately-for-a-successful-transition-to-agile-product-management/)

What Happens to Product Managers When Organizations Go Agile
(http://www.rallydev.com/community/agile-blog/what-happens-product-managers-when-organizations-go-agile)

What I Wish I Would Have Known When I Transitioned to Agile Product Management
(http://www.rallydev.com/community/agile-blog/what-i-wish-i-would-have-known-when-i-transitioned-agile-product-management)

The Gift of Meaningful Work

By Zach Nies

Have you ever been part of a company where it feels as though your value to the organization decreases as the organization grows? It seems that within growing companies there reaches a point where members of the original team leave (or are asked to leave) because the perception of their value seems to diminish.

I recently witnessed this at a highly successful tech company. When I joined, the founder was leading a product management group that was responsible for about $250 million in revenue. His product vision and ability to write software were key reasons why the company held its dominant position in the market. Repeatable large-scale execution wasn't his passion or gift, but like most technical founders, he was an amazing innovator.

About a year after the company went public, the founder was asked to step down from his position. In the maelstrom of execution as a public company, senior management considered him a risk. Why was this? While everyone else was focused on removing obstacles that got in the way of making quarterly numbers, his strength was on future-looking vision and innovation. Sadly, when companies place too much emphasis on quarterly and annual execution, future-looking people and products become liabilities.

The Innovator's Dilemma

To understand this notion, you must recognize the few key shifts that occur when a company's first product goes mainstream and is the source of significant revenue:

- Innovation seems like speculative investment in the future and thus it decreases
- The inertia of success tends to run over anything that can't prove its value in the immediate quarter or quarters
- The culture tends to shift from embracing uncertainty to embracing repeatable execution
- More emphasis is put on executing what's already working than on figuring out what's going to work

In effect, the company moves away from embracing ambiguity and innovation, and focuses instead on the steady, efficient execution of products that guarantee quarterly results. This may appear to be great—assuming that what has worked in the past continues to be effective—but most of the time it becomes deadly. As more companies continue to disrupt the market, the organizations that stay put—that stop innovating—will become less and less relevant.

Last year, two important books were published to help balance the tension between immediate portfolio execution and long-term innovation: *Escape Velocity*, by Geoffrey Moore, and *The Lean Startup*, by Eric Ries. Geoffrey Moore offers guidance on how to manage three investment horizons to ensure your company's future. A great complement to this view, Eric Ries provides a framework for navigating the extreme uncertainty inherent in new product and new market development.

Both books give new product and market creators language for making future-looking business cases to execution-oriented people. They also create a compelling framework for portfolio planning. Their combined wisdom offers fantastic insight into the value of acting differently, thinking about portfolio steering in a new way, and inviting innovation back into organizations.

Escaping the "pull of the past"

In *Escape Velocity*, for example, Moore introduces us to the McKinsey concept of three different time horizons for a business portfolio strategy. The horizons help us see past the common pitfalls of managing a portfolio by showing the relationship between investment and the timeframe of return.

Horizon 1:

Investments are expected to contribute to material returns in the same fiscal year in which they are brought to market, thereby generating today's cash flow.

Horizon 2:

Investments are expected to pay back significantly, but not in the year of their market launch. Typically, they are fast-growing from birth but come off a small base and need time to reach a material size, and so they demand patience.

Horizon 3:

Investments here are made in future businesses that will pay off years beyond the current planning horizon. They are not expected to appear in-market during the current planning year, and while they make claims against R&D budgets, they do not affect the go-to-market operating plan.

Moore suggests that considering these horizons in the steering of your portfolio will enable you to "escape the pull of the past" and drive next-generation growth from new lines of business. I believe this is key to being a successful Agile company with both a future-growth product strategy and a strong culture of people who remain proud and engaged.

Horizons Interpreted

A young startup working to put itself on the map lives mostly in Horizon 3. Here, it's all about learning: learning what the customer looks like and learning what product or service will inspire them to get their wallet out. Planning is still important in this Horizon, but the emphasis should be put on learning instead of sticking steadfastly to a plan.

In Horizon 2, things are starting to work. A product is meeting a market need and has begun to generate some revenue, but it hasn't hit a tipping point yet. There's still a lot of opportunity to learn and even moments where it may seem as though the company is taking steps backward in the market. Horizon 2 performance is typically measured by some combination of internal milestones, market indicators of tipping points, and revenue.

Horizon 1 is all about executing on the repeatable game plan developed in the previous two Horizons. The company has shown that by spending more, it can predict marginal increases in revenue. Success is now measured by typical performance metrics: planning and predicting future revenue and executing to results. This can be a scary place for people who have difficulty working this way, primarily innovators. It's no wonder why many leave or are asked to leave during this Horizon.

People who embrace and excel at uncertainty should lead forward-looking work. Consider the original team who initially led the company through Horizons 2 and 3. These are great people to take off of Horizon 1 work and focus instead on the speculative work of inventing the company's future.

Success and Survival
Inventing the future isn't easy or without its casualties. According to 2011's Startup Genome Report more than 90% of startups fail. But thanks to their significant foothold in existing markets, large companies generally have an advantage. Still, this advantage creates two big challenges:

- Horizon 2 and 3 work will be expected not to disrupt any current activity. This can be a hard pill to swallow.
- Horizon 2 and 3 work may be subjected to inappropriate measures of progress based on a skeptical Horizon 1 mindset. The skeptics may view new product development as an unmeasurable art and therefore far too risky an investment.

Historically, Horizon 2 and Horizon 3 portfolio investments have been made with a very fragile agreement that goes something like this:

"Give us a chunk of money and an independent corner of the business to operate within and we will invent the future. Trust us."

This isn't fair to either side of the agreement. Eric Ries's Lean Startup process allows for a much healthier agreement across the Horizon 2 and 3 teams and the rest of the business. The conversation goes something like this:

"Give us secure resources, we don't need much. And give us the authority to run the team following the Lean Startup process using Agile development techniques. In return, we will constantly report on our progress using the metrics of Innovation Accounting. You can see our process and measure our progress. Through our continuous transparency, we will create trust in your investment in our part of the portfolio."

The key is making sure the execution side of the company understands the process you're following, because that is how they look at the world. They also need to value the new measures necessary to understand your progress.

Before Eric's book and the Lean Startup process, there wasn't great language to describe this shift in thinking. While most successful early entrepreneurs naturally understood this concept, they struggled to translate it into language that execution-oriented Horizon 1 people within larger organizations could appreciate. That's the brilliance of the Lean Startup: it works in early startups as well as within well-established companies.

A New Way of Thinking and Acting

The inertia of success can run over anything. You may find yourself having to prove your portfolio investment value every quarter, or your culture may shift from embracing uncertainty to embracing repeatable execution. To ensure your future you must create well-rounded teams across all Horizons.

Find a handful of your early employees and founders who may feel trapped executing the known playbook and focus their efforts on freeing your company from the pull of its past. Give them a sandbox where they can innovate, and empower them with a personal stake in the outcome. When you do this, you're not only giving these people the gift of meaningful work, you're investing in the future of your business.

How Large Organizations Can Act More Like Startups

By Ryan Martens

Over the years, we've found that large organizations can benefit greatly from much of the thinking emerging in the startup community. Tapping into the entrepreneurial mindset helps bigger companies eliminate waste and create the innovative solutions they need to stay competitive in today's markets. What's more, combining many of the processes often used in the startup community can create a powerful whole solution.

Business Model Canvas, made popular by author and business advisor Alex Osterwalder and his team, is one such process. In his book *Business Model Generation*, Osterwalder shows how this highly visual tool often serves as a replacement for business plans for many startups. The tool, which can be used for visualization, analysis, design, and strategy, is quickly becoming common in large, established businesses as well.

Not only has the Business Model Canvas spurred a community of followers and innovators around the world, it has become an integral part of the Lean Startup movement—a concept developed by Eric Ries in 2011 as a way to bring a continuous flow of innovation into an organization.

Lean Startup marries Agile development with Silicon Valley entrepreneur Steve Blank's customer development approach to test and expose the relative value of different business models, and solutions on customer segments. It helps Agile teams prioritize how to increment their way through a large problem space. For new business/development efforts, this is typically done through close measurement of customer acquisition costs, funnel conversions, and revenue velocity.

The Business Model Canvas becomes the tool for managing the iterations of new business opportunities through a rapid three-phase process: build, measure, and learn. This disciplined, visible, and Agile approach has the power to help create high-impact and valuable solutions to businesses in all industries, not just for the software industry.

The Minimum Viable Product
By Todd Olson

What is the absolute minimum you need to build to understand whether you have a viable business proposition? How little can you spend to test your theories? These are precisely the questions raised when creating a Minimum Viable Product (MVP).

The goal behind an MVP, a concept popularized in Eric Ries's *The Lean Startup*, is to build the smallest possible product to validate the business or product concept. You want to spend as little as possible to stimulate learning and enter the Build-Measure-Learn loop that's an integral part of running a Lean Startup.

Sometimes an MVP requires manual processes or technology decisions that you know are not optimal, which can discourage larger organizations from building them. But an MVP should be thought of as a learning tool, not a final product. As long as you're learning from the MVP, it is doing its job.

At Rally Software, we wanted to build a new product in an adjacent market, Portfolio Management, based on customer feedback. We had some theories on the desired features, but we knew that we needed to validate our theories with customers. We were lucky to stumble upon an open-source Portfolio Management application built by one of our customers. We quickly leveraged the open-source project, and with a little bit of added work we were able to deliver a working prototype to customers within three weeks of our decision.

Leveraging the customer development process, we spent the next year continuing to evolve our MVP to learn more about customer desires. We updated it nearly weekly for a year until we validated (or invalidated) our theories and the PPM market. Then we rebuilt and launched the product using technology consistent with our production-quality products.

It's important to ask yourself these questions when building your MVP: Do I need this feature? What am I trying to learn? Is there an easier or cheaper way to learn this? How will I capture or measure what I learn? Once you have the answers you'll be well on your way to running your Lean Startup.

Start with Why

By Rachel Weston Rowell

Think for a moment about somebody you consider to be a leader. Whether that person is part of your personal or professional life, choose somebody whose ideas and actions drive a deep inspiration. Now think about why you react with such passion.

On the surface, you may be thinking about the reputation this person has earned or the work he or she has accomplished. Perhaps you're impressed by this leader's work or impact in the world. While these are all important measures of accomplishment, leadership comes from something much deeper than impact and achievement.

What is it about this person that inspires you? What is it that draws you to them? I'll give you a clue: it's not the what; it's the why.

In his book *Start with Why*, Simon Sinek argues that true leadership comes not from WHAT one does or HOW one does it, but WHY one does it in the first place. A leader doesn't need to incentivize, convince, or manipulate followers. Instead, this person leads with inspiration.

Inspired by the Golden Ratio, the Golden Circle is Sinek's mechanism for helping us understand the motivation, the why, behind what we do. And what's surprising about this model is that it starts from the inside out.

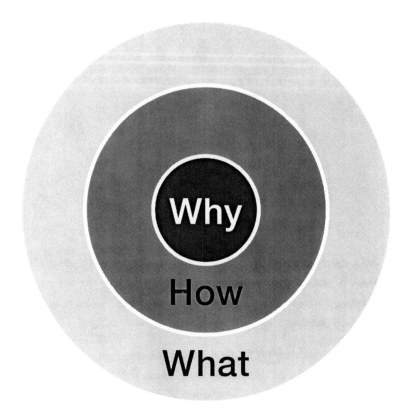

The "Golden Circle" from Simon Sinek

The Apple Advantage

In business, the "what"—the product or service—is often where much of the energy is placed, but that doesn't align with how people actually make purchasing decisions. Take Apple, for instance. Sinek points out that it's not Apple's product or method of delivery that has people lining up overnight. It's their why.

What Apple is really selling, and what people are buying, is a challenge to the status quo. An opportunity to be part of a group that "Thinks Different." And this WHY means that we won't stop at buying a computer from Apple. We will buy phones, mp3 players, tablets, and even music from the company. We will wait for hours in line. We will follow blogs and obsessively search for leaks of top-secret information. We are fans. Would you say the same of customer relationships to Dell or Motorola or Samsung?

Why WHY Matters

If you're not thinking about the WHY of your business, you simply aren't working with a complete set of data. And you are at serious risk of becoming a commodity, another "me too" play in a sea of sameness.

As you begin to think about an Agile transformation, it's important to consider what role you'll play and how you will lead your organization through this transformation. You could try incentives, coercion, even manipulation, but you'll see real success if you can inspire your organization with a powerful WHY.

What inspires them to follow you? Now you're getting closer to the WHY.

For more on the power of WHY, check out the video "Simon Sinek: How Great Leaders Inspire Action" on TED.com.

Story Mapping
By Eric Willeke

Have you ever used software that left you feeling the developers gave no thought to how it would actually be used, leaving you to figure it out on your own? If so, then you already know that providing a coherent experience is one of the keys to engaging users and creating successful products.

The quickest way to fix this is to maintain the user's perspective while laying out work for your teams—but this isn't easy when you're deep in a project. Unfortunately, with so many technical details to worry about, the coherence of a user's experience is often lost when working on complex projects.

Story Mapping, a method originally developed by Agile thought leader Jeff Patton, is a solution commonly used by Agile teams to address this challenge and create software that people can actually use.

Story Mapping always starts with "why." Clear articulation of the user's goal is the first and most powerful step, and should be reflected all the way through your backlog. From there, you must describe the journey users must take in order to achieve their goal. Don't worry about the details just yet. Instead, focus on clearly articulating the key actions and experiences for users as a series of high-level steps. This is generally captured as a horizontal row of sticky notes across the top of a large whiteboard or conference table.

Next, take a careful look at each step and decide what unanticipated needs your user might have. Write each of those detailed interactions on a card using the following format: "As <type of user>, I want to <specific action> so that <related goal or subgoal>." Place the card underneath the high-level step it supports, ideally using a different color card than the column header. Now think about what could go wrong for the user during that step, and add similarly formatted cards for the edge cases.

At this point, you have clearly visualized a portion of your product and developed much of the context needed for people to build it. Now it's up to you. Build a story map for your next key user journey and feel the difference it makes for your team and your users.

Information Radiators

By Eric Willeke

My least favorite professional moments have almost all been the result of an easily preventable error. Too often, I see problems arise simply because one or two people didn't know a critical detail that others assumed was obvious. As a result, I now consider *awareness* one of the keys to building successful teams and organizations.

When you implement a few simple tools to encourage awareness, quality improvements begin to occur. We call these tools *information radiators*.

When setting up information radiators, your first consideration should be what to make visible. I generally start with the three important aspects of a project that I want people to know:

First, I determine the goals of a project. It's critical that everybody has a shared understanding of the motivations and desired outcomes. This information too often gets buried in a project charter that only stakeholders and project managers read.

Second, I make sure everyone has visibility to the work that's in progress. This generally leads people to avoid mistakes by talking about dependencies before they turn into problems.

Finally, I ensure the whole team is acutely aware of any impediments that may affect the success of the project. Confronting people with these challenges leads to a much quicker resolution and makes the challenges impossible to ignore.

When displaying these information radiators, it's most effective to have them be on large, physical objects in highly trafficked places. A common example is to hang a flip-chart-sized poster in the break room or on a wall people regularly pass. For things that change frequently or have viewers in multiple locations, I lean toward an electronic system.

When you begin testing these ideas, you'll see how quickly people interact with them and begin naturally aligning their goals. Try it with your team and watch what happens.

Paper Prototyping
By Stephanie Tanner

It may seem challenging to find the time or the budget to test your designs within an Agile workplace. Make validating hypotheses quick and inexpensive through a technique known as *paper prototyping*.

A paper prototype is, simply, your planned user interaction drawn on paper. To try this technique, find a few users or colleagues and ask them to perform a task using your paper design. As they interact with your prototype by pointing or pressing on hand-drawn "buttons" or "links," place a piece of paper in front of them that represents the next action. This may be a wireframe drawing of the next screen or may just have a couple words to represent which screen displays next.

Ask your users specific questions about their experience with your prototype. For example: "What do you expect to happen when you click that link?" As you collect the real-time feedback, make notes on the paper with their questions and suggestions. For the next user, you may choose to use a fresh copy or an updated paper prototype that incorporates the suggestions made by previous participants.

While this method can be effective, paper prototyping does come with a few challenges. The nature of the process (pen and paper) is best done face-to-face; it's difficult to test a paper prototype remotely. Another downside to paper prototyping is the difficulty of describing complex interactions on paper. The technique is ideal for information architecture decisions, page layouts, simple dialogues, and other click events. It is not recommended for drag-and-drop, mouse-over interactions, auto-completions, and other tasks that require more involved interactions.

But even with its challenges, paper prototyping is a valuable technique that can be carried out with ease and speed.

2
Build the Thing Right

Build the Thing Right

By Bob Gower

You can't have great software without a great team, and most software teams behave like dysfunctional families.

—Jim McCarthy

I once spent a week consulting at a company that was on the verge of falling apart. In the six months prior to my arrival, three quarters of its development team had turned over, not a single piece of new code had been released, and no one on the technology team would commit to a timeline for getting even simple updates of the product into customer hands.

The business people were frustrated—actually they were openly angry—and were making commitments to customers without the consent of the technology team. They, of course, then used those commitments to berate, cajole, and openly threaten the developers, saying in effect that "we'll lose *major customer x* and go out of business if *YOU* don't deliver." The technology team responded passive-aggressively. They would complain in private and then try to do the best they could, even giving up precious personal time to try to meet the unreasonable deadlines. But still, their hearts weren't in it.

If you think this sounds like a formula for business failure, you're right. If you think this sounds unusual, you are unfortunately wrong. This situation was remarkable only to the degree things were falling apart—the dynamics themselves are all too common.

Slow Down to Speed Up

In order to understand where things went wrong and where the opportunities to fix these missteps lie, we must go back to the telling statement I made at the beginning of the story: no one on the technology team would commit to a timeline. The casual reader might think the team members were unskilled or just obstinate and lazy—the conclusion the business team came to—but in reality there was something deeper going on.

Like most teams I encounter, this one was made up of hardworking people who really wanted to do a good job. They certainly didn't want to be yelled at or be forced to work nights and weekends, though that is exactly what was happening. If there had been a simple way out of this mess they would have happily taken it, but unfortunately there wasn't.

They were working with an application that had been in production for more than 10 years. The product was so poorly coded and maintained that touching any part of it would often cause something to break in another seemingly unrelated area. And because the developers had no automated test coverage—they couldn't just push a button and run a full-system test to see if anything broke—it was often customers who found the new problem *after* the code had been released.

While to the business people it looked as though the IT folks were being difficult, in reality they were being responsible. They honestly couldn't commit to a date—at least not one that was palatable to their handlers—because there were simply too many unknowns in the process. The fact that most of them were new to the product certainly didn't help matters either.

All of this illustrates a simple truth: if you want to go fast, you must first be willing to go slowly.

If this company had originally made a commitment to build the product right, it would not have been in this situation. Now the only option was to stop all development of new features—thus losing the race with the competition—and overhaul the system, or to muddle on until the increasing defects in the system collapsed the whole thing. Both options are difficult to swallow.

Pulling Quality Forward

If we're going to build businesses that can survive chaotic markets and produce sustained value for customers and shareholders, it's important that we build things right the first time. While it may be tempting to sacrifice quality for short-term gain, that is almost always a bad long-term business decision. At the very least, it's a decision that should be made consciously and strategically, not because there isn't enough time to do things right.

If we're going to make a commitment to building things right, we must first understand some important key elements. Most important, we must shift from a mindset of inspection to prevention. In other words, we should focus not on fixing defects but on making products devoid of defects in the first place. This is essential if we wish to practice Continuous Integration or Continuous Delivery.

How then do we as business people support this?

Building a System that Builds It Right

While there are many practices and tools that we can put in place to support writing defect-free code, the most essential is an insistence on teamwork. Our products are complex, and without coordinated effort things will go wrong. And of course the best place to coordinate work is with the people actually doing the work. This means they need to talk to each other and feel like part of a team.

We can further support their ability to do great work if we create an environment where they pull work from a prioritized queue, rather than have work assigned to them.

A team whose members pull business requirements, then decide together how they will solve the problem, is motivated and engaged and will produce great work. In an environment like this, there are few surprises, and mistakes tend to get caught early. What's more, there is a sense that work is collectively owned, which leads to greater cooperation and collaboration. Rather than QA finding bugs in the developer's code, both parties work together to ensure that the entire team is producing high-quality work.

Taking things a step further, this working style allows the QA team to get the requirement first and develop automated tests even before the code is written (Test Driven Development, or TDD). This means that we develop a system that can be fully tested at the push of a button and we can quickly determine whether the new thing we are adding to the system is breaking something already in production.

Over time, this new way of working leads to a more agile, stable, and valuable organization, capable of withstanding a volatile and fickle market. By building things right the first time, we create a high-performance machine capable of sudden maneuvers.

In this section we'll delve a bit deeper into this philosophy and identify some of the practices and tools you can start using today to make your product and business the best they can be.

Agile Test and Engineering Practices
By Chris Browne

Traditionally in the software world, it fell to teams of humans to perform complex, repetitive activities such as building code and deploying it to customers. But humans are error prone and tend to be quite slow. We were able to get by, though not without considerable overhead, lengthy lead times, and high stress levels. The significant effort and expense involved in ensuring the quality of our product and getting it into customers' hands meant we did it rather infrequently.

But times have changed and now it's possible, with some planning and discipline, to drop the cost of these formerly expensive activities close to zero. And as the need to beat competitors to market and respond quickly to customer requests or competitive disadvantages has increased, decreasing our time to market becomes more essential to our success. We simply can't afford to take months or even weeks to deliver a defect fix or new feature to a waiting customer. We need to adapt our processes, practices, and tools to provide the flexibility to deliver value to our customers at will.

In order to improve quality and decrease the amount of overhead required to get working software into our customers' hands, we must remove the human element from complex, repeatable, and expensive tasks. By automating build, test, and deployment activities, we are able to establish a safe environment in which we can experiment and focus on our strength: innovating problem solving and design.

Automation is only part of the answer. We also need to change the way we validate design decisions and share information by collaborating more often and earlier in the process. If we focus on technical excellence and good design while committing to share information and improve our practices, we're able to gradually move to a deliver-at-will model with excellent quality and customer satisfaction.

Below you'll find some ideas for how you might start investing in technical practices that will enhance your Agility:

Automated Testing

Automating tests is one of the most valuable steps you can take as part of your Agile transition. Although the initial cost of creating an automated test is typically higher than its manual counterpart, all subsequent test runs are much quicker and cheaper. Once run times and testing costs decrease, running these tests regularly becomes a more viable option.

When a full regression takes weeks to complete, the natural reaction is to perform them infrequently, but what if it only took 15 minutes? How would that change your developers' behavior? How would it allow you to better support your customers?

Different types of automated tests are valuable for different reasons:

Unit Tests

A unit test is implemented to verify an independent unit of code. Unit tests are typically the first automated tests to run as part of an automated build because they run very quickly and can provide the developer with immediate feedback regarding potential issues. A comprehensive unit test suite makes it easy to re-factor or make large sweeping changes to an application; it acts as a safety net in case the change had unintended consequences elsewhere in the codebase.

Integration Tests

An integration test is used to confirm that related parts of an application are interacting with each other as intended. Integration test execution typically follows the successful completion of a unit test run as part of an automated build process. These more complex tests run after unit tests since they take longer to complete due to setup costs and communication delays between components.

Automated Acceptance Tests

An acceptance test verifies the functionality that was added to the product from the user's perspective. In a user story, when acceptance test criteria have been defined before the code is implemented, they can help validate that the developer's implementation is functionally correct. Once these acceptance tests have been automated, they can be run repeatedly in the future at low cost to ensure the user's experience has not been disrupted.

Performance/Load Tests

Performance tests help to ensure the stability of the product by simulating different levels of load or spikes in activity. By testing the performance of changes added to the product, you can prevent a significant degradation in your users' experience due to a lack of responsiveness or system availability. Since performance tests often simulate multiple-user interaction with an application over longer periods of time, they typically run last and represent the final sanity check before a product can be released to your customers.

All the automated testing types listed above help reduce the need for manual testing and can significantly decrease the number of defects that escape to your customers. The more test automation you employ, the more time your testers and developers can spend delivering value to your customers.

Continuous Integration, Automated Builds, and Automated Deployments

Along with test automation, you should also start looking at how often you integrate, build, and deploy code, and how long each activity takes.

Continuous integration is the process of very regularly integrating small changes into a product rather than trying to stitch a large number of changes together at once. In order for continuous integration to work, it's essential to have automated your build and test processes so that each change can be validated immediately. This allows you to identify potential issues and mistakes earlier in the product development lifecycle so plans can be adjusted if necessary.

Just like automated testing, automating your build process is going to save engineers time. The process of building a deployable software package is highly complex and time consuming, and thus prone to mistakes. By investing in the creation of build scripts or tools you can mitigate the risk of builds failing due to human error and enable developers to focus on more important tasks.

Automation only really works if you treat it as a first-class citizen. Automated tests that are consistently in a failing state or automated builds that don't regularly complete are useless and often ignored.

Automating the deployment process has benefits as well. If you make it easy to deploy code, people no longer have to wait to test, which saves time. According to Steve Neely, a Rally software engineer, "If you run tests, build code, or deploy software frequently, you get more practice and have the opportunity to improve upon your processes more often."

Collaboration

A focus on the human element for non-repeatable, creative tasks like code creation and design also helps increase the quality of your products. Activities such as pair programming and code reviews will help developers collaboratively validate their design decisions by getting more eyes on the solution. Practicing test-driven development can result in simpler, more elegant designs, and can minimize rework. This helps ensure all parties are on the same page and have thought through the design together prior to beginning any real development.

Scrum and Kanban

By Rick Simmons

When we talk about Agile, we often talk about Scrum or Kanban, the two dominant flavors of Agile practice. To better understand Agile values and principles, and how they get expressed in the real world with real projects, it's important to understand some of the details of these two frameworks.

Scrum

For the past 50 years in technology, we all have witnessed similar challenges: too much work, constant changes, late delivery, low predictability. These are the problems that Agile was developed to solve, and its accelerating adoption is indicative that it works. According to Forrester Research, Inc., more than 40% of companies have adopted Agile practices.

Scrum (*Scrum* is a copyright of the Scrum Alliance for their iterative software development framework) is the most widely adopted form of Agile. It has been in use for more than 15 years and has been employed in many types of technology work, from pure software to mixed hardware/software and embedded systems development, and to many "knowledge work" areas outside of technology.

It helps teams produce higher-quality work that better meets stakeholder needs, and do so in a more predictable way. While Scrum is easy to understand, it can be challenging to master.

Scrum is made up of just a few simple roles, events, and artifacts, but it relies on the collaborative efforts of individuals to create specific agreements and policies, and to maintain the discipline needed to realize its potential.

One of the most important ideas in Scrum is that it puts teams in control: they make the decisions about how to organize, prioritize, and execute their work. Scrum teams are made up of 5 to 10 people and include everyone needed to produce the output. This often includes designers, developers, testers, and sometimes people with specialized skills as well, such as architect, technical writer, or release engineer.

The teams work in small timeboxes, called Sprints or iterations, of two or sometimes four weeks. Inside this timebox, they do all of the work needed to fully develop and test a small increment of a larger project. We call this increment "potentially releasable" because, while we might not actually release it to the customer, it is fully tested, reliable, and able to be demonstrated. This lets us interact with stakeholders so we can get real-time feedback, which ultimately helps us build a better product.

Scrum teams always include one person who is accountable for making the right business decisions about the priority of work that gets executed in the Sprint. Called the Product Owner, or PO, this person focuses mainly on the Product Backlog, which is the list of all the work needed to build the product or complete the project. The PO normally writes the "user stories" that populate the backlog, and works with stakeholders and team members to elaborate them and to develop acceptance criteria.

In addition to the team and the PO, Scrum defines one more critical role: the ScrumMaster, or SM. The SM acts as a servant leader, facilitating meetings and retrospectives, protecting the team from interruptions, and removing impediments that stand in the way. She may also collect metrics data and help coordinate work between multiple Scrum teams who are working on a common project. What the SM never does is make decisions about the work or how things are going to get built, or assign work to individuals or make commitments for the team.

How Scrum Works

The flow of work in Scrum is very simple.

First, there is the ongoing work of maintaining or "grooming" the backlog, and this is mostly the PO's focus. However, the whole team collaborates in an ongoing fashion and is responsible for estimating the stories.

At the start of the Sprint, the PO and team, often facilitated by the SM, holds a Sprint planning meeting. This occurs on the first day of the Sprint and lasts from four to eight hours. The purpose of this meeting is to prioritize the work, clarify objectives, and plan the details of the Sprint. This is mostly the work of the team members, who make all the critical decisions. But the PO has final authority on the priority of individual work items.

During the Sprint, the team members work diligently to make progress. They meet daily in a 15-minute Scrum or standup meeting, where they communicate with one another about the progress of the work and describe any impediments. The PO answers questions about specific work items as needed. The team members also keep track of the amount of work remaining, so they can be confident in their ability to achieve the goal within the Sprint timebox. Scrum uses burn-down charts and Cumulative Flow Diagrams for quick visual feedback on the progress of the Sprint.

The Sprint concludes with a Sprint Review and Retrospective on the last day. The Review is a short open meeting during which the team demonstrates what it has produced and shares the accomplishments and challenges encountered during the Sprint. This provides visibility to the organization as well as critical feedback to the team and the PO.

Once the Review is complete, the team holds a Retrospective, a core aspect of Scrum that is focused on improvement. The Retro is a private meeting for the team, the PO, and the SM. It lasts anywhere from two to eight hours, depending on the length of the Sprint and other factors. The team discusses the Sprint and considers ways to improve how it works. The SM plays a key role in helping a team through the Retro process and supporting team members as needed in the larger organization.

The Retro brings the team full-cycle back to the launch of the next Sprint and creates the path to continuous improvement—a concept at the heart of Agile.

Kanban

One size definitely doesn't fit all, and as successful as timebox-based Agile approaches have been, they aren't optimal for all circumstances. The Kanban Method provides alternative approaches for teams that find the broad process changes that Scrum requires to be too disruptive, or that struggle with some aspects of the Scrum framework.

Kanban (the *Kanban Method* is in the process of being formalized by Lean-Kanban University) is about identifying opportunities for improvement in how a team works and finding ways to introduce change in a focused and incremental way. In addition, it provides a simple and extremely effective approach for visualizing and managing the work of a team.

In Kanban, we create a simple model of how work flows in a particular context. An example might be: Ready to Start—Designing—Building—Testing—Done. Then we draw a representation of this model on a white-board or in an electronic tool. This consists of columns that represent the work states. Each work item is written on a card and flows across the board as work progresses. The board and cards are governed by simple policies that the team develops, which describe how work flows, what each state means, and how cards are prioritized. The Kanban board visualization is a powerful tool for communicating the status and flow of work. It also high-lights where bottlenecks are so the team can address points of congestion or blockage and get work flowing again.

The objective of a Kanban system is the smooth and predictable flow of work through the team. Once a work item is started, team members focus fero-ciously on getting it done, and always try to favor finishing one thing before starting another. This is because Kanban recognizes a universal fact: working on too many things simultaneously slows the completion of everything.

Kanban teams pay close attention to "Cycle Time" (also referred to as "Lead Time"), the actual time it takes for a piece of work to get done in its entirety. Teams set explicit "Work in Process" (WIP) limits on the number of work items that are "live" at any one time, which are meant to represent the capacity of the team and to strike a balance between a reasonable workload and maintaining the flexibility to work efficiently. These are among the key ways that we reduce Cycle Time, since working on fewer things lets us get the other things done more quickly.

Kanban teams rapidly develop an understanding of how long it takes to complete work items and are always looking for possible steps to reduce this time (e.g. through better collaboration or automation). Kanban metrics leverage this knowledge to foster greater responsiveness and better expectation-setting with stakeholders. They also provide a clear sense of capacity, or the number of work items that can flow through the team in a certain amount of time, which we express as Throughput.

Because we create the Kanban board model based on how the team currently works, we can accommodate things like specialized roles, hand-offs to outside parties, work that needs to be expedited through the team, and other unique situations. By prioritizing and tackling work in a continuous flow, we are always free to choose the next item based on current priorities.

Kanban is especially good at pointing out the most valuable opportunities to improve how we work. When work gets stalled on the board, Kanban teams will swarm on the problem to get work flowing again and will try to find ways to prevent the problem from happening again. This "guided improvement" is a fundamental aspect of Kanban and is very effective in helping a team or organization improve in small increments, which over a longer term can create dramatic improvements in capability and predictability.

These aspects of visualization, WIP limits, policies, flow, measurement, and improvement are at the core of the Kanban Method and constitute a framework that accommodates a wide range of work situations.

Scrum *or* Kanban?

By Rick Simmons

Making decisions about process is difficult and imperfect, which is why Agile requires teams to constantly inspect and adapt their methods based on their own experiences. But everyone has to start somewhere, and that is true when choosing an Agile framework. For many, this means choosing between Scrum and Kanban.

It's important to realize that most aspects of Scrum and Kanban are compatible. Both approaches require ongoing experimentation and improvement, and virtually all Agile teams end up combining aspects of different frameworks.

Scrum works well in organizations that benefit from the "forced discipline" of defined planning and feedback cycles. It provides a fairly complete process definition that includes roles, activities, events, and artifacts. Many organizations benefit from this more prescriptive approach to work management, operating in timeboxes where work is fully planned at the start.

Kanban provides a more incremental approach to work management and improvement. Organizations that have a lot of on-demand work that can't wait for the next planning cycle to begin, or work that involves hand-offs, sign-offs, or significant waiting periods, often find Kanban's continuous flow approach to be a better fit. Kanban is also effective for processes that involve numerous specialized roles, long delivery cycles, large work items, or pipelined activities. And it has proven to be very effective for teams whose main concern is the oversight or coordination of the work of others.

Remember that your process will evolve to become unique to your needs, and this is the most fundamental strength of Agile.

Reciprocal Commitment
By Eric Willeke

All Agile methods require the team to offer a commitment, whether it's an iteration commitment, date commitment, or service-level agreement. Unfortunately, organizations often ignore the fact that these commitments always go two ways, from business to team, and team to business.

In the role of Product Owner you make a commitment to the team members each and every time you ask them to make a commitment to you. When you honor your commitment to provide a stable working environment, you are enabling the team to trust your word and effectively accomplish its work. In turn, this vastly improves the likelihood that you will receive the desired outcome, thus allowing you to deliver against your longer-term plans.

Any business relationship is a partnership, and very few are closer than the relationship between the Product Owner and a team. Despite the separation of roles, you and your team will either succeed or fail *together*.

Every partnership requires a strong commitment from both parties, and software development is no different. These commitments take many forms. In Agile methods, there is an implied commitment that the organization makes to the team: "We will allow you to function as a team, and will not continually disrupt you by adding and removing team members."

Additionally, staffing managers and line managers are expected to commit to their direct reports who are members of teams: "I will not micromanage your work as part of the team; I trust you to be a professional."

Finally, and of most importance to Product Owners, there is the commitment you're making to the team: "I will not change the intent or priority of this work for the next two weeks."

In exchange, your team should offer you a commitment to deliver an agreed-upon work product to you within the next two weeks, per the definition of done that we published and agreed to respect.

This commitment makes you vulnerable to your team, as its members can hold you to it despite your desire to change. It exposes you within your organization, as you are required to make your intent explicit for everybody to see. It empowers you to look forward, strengthens your integrity, and drives results. This commitment is powerful, and it deserves to be presented explicitly and honored by you and your team.

Make your commitment, make it clear, and only then ask for a commitment in return.

Enjoy the trust and the results that emerge.

The Art of the Hackathon

By Charles Ferentchak

At Rally we're always striving to improve, and our internal hackathons ensure that we never stop improving.

A hackathon is a short and intense code-writing session. During these sessions, developers try to create a project or solve a specific problem. These events are usually stocked with everything a developer needs to get code written with as few distractions as possible. Hackathons are common in the developer world and most engineers find them to be a fun and interesting way to spend a few days tinkering with new ideas. But these events are not *just* about having fun; there are a handful of benefits that come from hosting an internal hackathon.

For example, one of our Rally developers understood the pain that our newer employees experienced in setting up their computers to work on our system. This engineer spent a short period of time creating a standardized program that new engineers could use to customize their systems. Previously, engineers may have spent up to a week setting up their own machine. In the end, it was a hackathon that helped save our engineering organization weeks of wasted time.

Hackathons are also a great chance for developers to use advanced technology to create new features. As a developer myself, I've often wished for a better or faster way to make a specific feature. Software is complex stuff and there is no better way to explain it than to build a prototype and show it off. Hackathons empower developers to explore beyond their normal routine and innovate from within.

The most important part of a hackathon is to reduce outside interference and restrictions. Let developers be creative and make sure they have everything they need to be successful. We've found that when we provide our teams the best technology we can find and give them permission to be as creative as they want (and supply beer and snacks of course) the ideas begin to flow.

If your developers are anything like ours, a hackathon will give them the freedom they need to remove the obstacles that are getting in the way and to start solving problems in fresh new ways.

Agile Metrics

By Isaac Montgomery

If applied correctly, metrics can be a powerful tool to inform and empower your success. And metrics misapplied can deal a crippling blow to the very things you are really wanting to measure—the productivity and health of your product and organization.

To successfully apply any metric, you must understand what you're measuring and why you're measuring it in the first place.

Because every measurement will have an effect on the individuals, teams, and organizations being measured—whether the effect is intentional or otherwise—you must learn to ask the kinds of questions that reveal your true purpose.

Is your intent to assess performance? To set targets? To reward your best and motivate your least productive people? If so, consider that you tend to get that which you measure, not necessarily the intent of that measure.

> **Example**: I recently worked with an organization that set an arbitrary target for its teams to increase their throughput by 25% each quarterly release. It worked. Every team met the target. After a year the average estimated size of a work item grew by 70%—estimated, not actual.

Is your intent to enforce consistency or assess conformance to standards? If that's the case, consider whether or not consistency is truly a virtue and whether enforced standards are the best way to encourage use of valuable practices.

> **Example**: A few years ago, I worked with a well-intentioned development director who believed passionately in automated testing (a passion I share). He required that all of his teams maintain a level where 90% of their software was covered by automated tests. Any team that fell below that standard would face a full-team code review and coaching session with the director. Teams rarely fell below the standard. And the rate of defects escaping into production steadily increased release after release.

Is your intent to learn and improve? To gain a better understanding of your capabilities? To facilitate experimentation and continuous improvement? To make visible what is working and what isn't?

> **Example**: One director I worked with was particularly passionate about pair programming—a critical Agile software development technique. She told me with great pride that after witnessing the great success one of her teams had with pairing, today all of her teams spend on average 25% of their time utilizing the technique.

The most effective metrics are those designed to generate the kind of insights that enable informed decision making and improved business outcomes. To be successful at understanding metrics, you must remember to always ask: What outcomes am I looking for? What decisions do I need to make? What insights will help me make those decisions?

Only once you've answered those important questions can you truly begin to identify what it is you wish to measure.

Continuous Integration and Delivery
By John Michael Martin

This spring I had a gig in Oklahoma City, and to get ready for the long stay I bought an eight-pack of soda. One by one, I placed the bottles upright into the door of the mini fridge in my hotel room. And when I had finished, do you know what happened? I couldn't close the door.

That's what continuous integration is for.

Continuous Integration (CI) is the practice of regularly verifying that the code you're working on will continue to work as expected when combined with the changes that everyone else on the team is making. There are tools that help with this. These tools poll the version control system and, once something has been checked in, get the code, compile it, and run the associated set of automated tests to ensure it works.

CI tools are useful, but CI is not just about the tool. CI is a mindset. In other words, it's not about the system; it's about the practice: What's the smallest thing I can do that can be measured in a way that gives me useful information to proceed?

Implementing a mindset of continuous verification has several benefits: it encourages making smaller, more easily verified changes; it generates and supports a test-early mentality, supports a test-early mentality, and generates a suite of useful test cases for later re-validation; it encourages the incremental delivery of small bits of value; it creates an environment in which I am constantly reminded that I am part of the team; and it's an addictive gateway to total code and quality ownership.

I was drawn to CI when I was the build guy on a project that did weekly drops to QA. We would schedule a code "freeze," build the software, and then deploy it to QA. The code freeze was supposed to be on Thursday night, but for a long time we had been operating under a different term: we called it a code "slush." So the freeze would creep into Friday, which was bad because it took an entire day to compile and deploy the code. This meant that I was running around like a crazed monkey late on Fridays, which was not a good way to launch into the weekend.

The problem was not that the code took several hours to compile—the code could compile in about fifteen minutes. The problem was in the practice. Somebody would tell me that the code was ready to build, and I'd kick it off. The build would immediately fail to compile and I'd spend the rest of the day tracking down the person who forgot to check a file in. Then it would fail again and I'd have to track someone else down who had made "a little change that shouldn't have affected anything." Then it would fail again and I'd have to work with the developer who realized that it successfully compiled in his environment because, for some reason, it took two passes to compile properly. Then it would fail again ...

So we installed and configured a CI system to conduct exactly one test. Every time a developer checked code into the source code control system, the CI server would detect it, get all the code, and rebuild. The failure/success check was: Did something get created? If not, then whoever checked in most recently would stop and figure out what they changed so they could make the build work again. If fifteen developers all checked in at the same time at the end of the week and something was missing, there were too many clues to sort through. If I was the only developer to check in after the last successful compile, then it was pretty clear that I'd be the one best suited to resolve the problem.

Within a few weeks, our process was down to an hour. It was a significant change because it meant that we could get stuff to QA faster without pushing work into the weekend. It also meant that the trouble-shooting of build failures was faster because the event that triggered the failure was isolated and easier to review—a bit like identifying patient zero in a small community.

Once that lesson seeped in, we jumped into adding automated testing to the mix to get even more feedback. After all, it was useful to know that the compile worked. But knowing that the system would continue to do what we expected of it after a change was made was even more valuable. Again, it's easier to pinpoint the problem if fewer changes occur between working and not working. Once we got used to that, we automated the deployment of the resulting product into a testing environment so that a suite of auto-mated functional tests could be run. Just six months after implementing the CI system, we had reduced the deployment and production release process from four days to two and a half hours.

Teams that want to get "better" get addicted to acquiring and reacting to feedback. And the opportunities to push further in both directions are growing. We discovered something that many new teams are discovering every day: the most effective way to get "better" is very often to get Agile.

The Value of Play

By John Michael Martin

Play is an important part of building productive teams.

Team members who share experiences, from taking classes to playing games together, receive myriad benefits, including a safe environment for debate, a shared foundation of assumptions, and a localized dialect—all of which are necessary to create a collaborative culture that resists lazy acquiescence and group-think. What's more, sharing experiences creates a unique team shorthand that can make communication more efficient.

For example, the people on my team know that if we're having a debate and I make a gesture that involves shaking my hand in the air, we need to discuss some of the underlying assumptions because I'm becoming overwhelmed by data input. This gesture was created after an experience we shared that taught us a little dance about the parts of the brain, and the gesture now serves as a tribe-building language shortcut.

But even though games are valuable, it's important not to impose games on your teams. There is a lot of (appropriate) resistance to cheesy, well-intentioned "team-building" games. Let your team members figure out what they like to play and give them the time and space to do so.

Encourage your teams to play by themselves. High-bandwidth engagement from your team members is another vital component to fast-paced development and accurate forecasting. Technical folks are explorers. Give them a chance to explore and experiment on your product, and they'll have a deeper understanding of the possibilities, find interesting new paths through the codebase, and develop a stronger connection to and interest in the product and your projects.

This winter, I took some time to play: I wrote a shooting gallery add-on for Rally's requirements-management tool. It's hardly anything we'd ever think of selling. However, it allowed me to find new areas of the UI framework I hadn't ever explored. A week later, a customer request actually required us to exercise that bit of the framework and, because I had spent that crucial time playing, I was 10 times more confident in my estimate for completion and ability to execute.

Flow

By Karl Scotland

Flow is the result of doing the thing right. It is the regular and smooth progress of work on a product from its initial concept to its final consumption.

Work that progresses in large chunks, in a stop-start manner, does not have flow. It's the work that progresses in small pieces, in a continuous manner, that ultimately creates the kind of flow your organization needs. By reducing completion time and enabling greater predictability and reliability, this kind of work builds trust and fosters creativity and innovation.

Moreover, reducing utilization and creating spare capacity, sometimes referred to as slack, improves our ability to respond to changes and surprises. After all, we don't run our servers at 100%, and we know how well traffic flows on a gridlocked road! This spare capacity is what gives us time to spend on continuous improvement and innovation.

Working on smaller and fewer pieces of work helps minimize delays and generates faster feedback. It's like operating a fast and nippy speedboat rather than a slow, sluggish cargo tanker. Further, balancing demand against capability, and not starting more work than you can complete, means that work isn't left hanging around and depreciating. Imagine the pileup caused by trying to push a chain of paperclips across a table versus the smooth flow created by pulling them across.

So how does an organization go about actually achieving flow? Focus on progressing and completing a smaller number of smaller pieces of work. Make that work, and its flow, visible in a physical shared place, and when work becomes blocked, encourage teams to resolve issues and concentrate on finishing that piece of work rather than starting something new. When aspects of the workflow are found to be progressing less quickly and smoothly than you would like, invest time in improving the workflow in order to develop future capability.

While this may appear to reduce the amount of time one is kept busy, it's important to remember that busyness and productivity are not the same thing.

Measuring activity, in terms of utilization, will not create great results. Instead of focusing on the worker, focus on the work product and measure work outcomes by things like throughput for productivity, lead time for responsiveness, and due-date performance for reliability. These are all appropriate measures of flow.

Stop starting and start finishing.

Tools

By Julie Byrne

If you're a leader in a software development organization, you may struggle at times to get an accurate picture of the development teams' status and progress. Looking for a solution? An Agile application lifecycle management (ALM) tool can provide the visibility executive management needs in order to effectively steer an organization.

Agile ALM is the management of the software development lifecycle from ideation through implementation. It provides a unified, real-time view of project-related data while also building and testing results.

Having a unified view of data in a single tool benefits an organization in many ways, including the ability to provide visibility for distributed teams where physical boards are not adequate. Additionally, real-time metrics, such as the iteration burndown, are automatically calculated, providing accurate team progress information.

Dashboards that aggregate productivity and quality metrics keep the entire team informed and help drive team conversations during planning sessions, daily standups, and iteration reviews and retrospectives.

Finally, Agile ALM tools facilitate program-level coordination across multiple teams. What's more, key stakeholders can view progress across a program or business unit to assess milestones, participation, and workflow.

And remember, tools alone do not make a team successful. According to the Agile Manifesto, one of the most important Agile core values is "Individuals and interactions over processes and tools." The data and metrics provided in an Agile ALM tool should be used to support Agile practices and encourage conversations, from the team level all the way up through executive management.

Why Define Done?

By Eric Willeke

The process of building software is inherently full of ambiguity. We never know exactly what we want in advance, and we strongly value the ability to make changes once the product is complete. This is what drives the use of Agile methods in our development efforts. However, one thing we do not value is failing to understand what we've actually received. This is where the definition of "done" comes into play. It removes a lot of the ambiguity around what it means for a team to say "We've finished this," allowing follow-up decisions to be made from a position anchored in reality.

This knowledge that completed work meets a certain set of standards provides the basis for trust in the partnership between a Product Owner and a team. Teams know their work will be accepted if it meets the product's needs. Teams even gain the ability to create a checklist to augment their professionalism and ease any regulatory burden.

On the other side of the partnership, the business and the team share a clear understanding about the quality of their product. When teams respect the definition of done, they understand it is a commitment; there's no longer room for additional work, however strong the desire.

The notion that there is no more additional work hiding beyond "done" is, in fact, crucial to creating the consistency Agile promises. If a standard for done isn't set and properly understood, it makes the schedule and the project itself almost impossible to quantify. Worse, teams aren't able to make meaningful commitments around their work. Thus, when teams honor the definition of done, they are able to demonstrate their integrity and professionalism.

Welcome to reality. The news isn't always good, but at least you know where you stand.

3

People, Not Resources

People, Not Resources

By Bob Gower

For me, this is a familiar image—people in the organization ready and willing to do good work, wanting to contribute their ideas, ready to take responsibility, and leaders holding them back, insisting that they wait for decisions or instructions.

—Margaret J. Wheatley

There is a supply-and-demand paradox brewing in the software business, and it's getting worse by the day. Every company I talk to is searching for rock-star talent, while at the exact same moment most of the talented people I come across are searching for great work.

People on both sides of this issue are frustrated—companies can't find the right workers, or enough of them, and talented workers feel stifled, bored, and in many cases exhausted, and even oppressed, by the work they do find.

It's an easy field for employers to stand out in, and yet so few fail to create the kind of engaging workplaces that attract top talent. Most blame their troubles on the market or a lack of money, but it's hard to take this argument seriously when Wikipedia attracted an army of volunteers with seemingly little effort, and then produced so much value it drove Microsoft's well-funded Encarta out of business. How did Wikipedia attract and motivate so much unpaid talent, and how does this hugely popular project keep doing it?

The secret to hiring top talent is simple—but not easy.

Most workplaces seem diabolically designed to kill creativity, intelligence, and productivity, and thus drive away talent. If you want to hire well, you need to first engage and inspire the talent you do have, and that's not about money. It's about treating people like people. It's a matter of helping them align toward a compelling common vision, giving them the tools and environments they need, then getting out of their way.

This is not only good karma, it's good business.

Fuzzy Guiding Principles

In 1986, Craig Reynolds, with his groundbreaking computer simulation BOIDS, discovered he could get a set of computer objects to "flock" like birds in ever-changing, emergent, beautiful patterns. He accomplished this not by programming each object's individual trajectory—a complicated, heavyweight, and defect-prone task—but by giving each object three simple rules:

- Separation: steer to avoid crowding local flockmates
- Alignment: steer toward the average heading of local flockmates
- Cohesion: steer to move toward the average position of local flockmates

It turns out that these simple rules, when applied to the system, allowed beautiful and complex behaviors to emerge. The same thing can happen in our organizations if we set the stage right and then get out of the way.

Command-and-control management, our business-as-usual system, is complicated, heavyweight, and defect-prone. It's much like trying to program the individual trajectory of each computer object. At best it creates a kind of begrudging compliance, and at worst belligerent opposition. And I've never seen this managerial style inspire true alignment or engagement, which is what we need if we are to stay competitive in increasingly dynamic and chaotic markets.

Instead of micromanaging hierarchical controls, we need simple rules, healthy environments, and ultimately dynamic cultures that encourage the emergence of complex and beautiful behaviors and products. The task of the modern manager and business builder, therefore, is much like that of an organic gardener—we create the conditions from which value can emerge, then stand out of the way and let nature take its course, always learning and adjusting the system when needed.

There are two points of influence for companies that want to encourage the growth and development of such dynamic systems: the structure of the organization, and the behavior of managers and leaders.

Structure

Structure includes tangible and explicit things like org charts, buildings, processes, and tools, and also intangibles like the habits and unspoken rules that govern "the way we do things around here."

My experience has led me to value a few things that can get baked in, or left out, of these structures. There are several, but I'll confine myself to the three most important:

Teams: An organizational structure based on small, cross-functional teams whose membership stays relatively consistent over time is, in my experience, essential. I don't mean a group of people with a loose affiliation. I mean a tight group whose members communicate daily, if not hourly—a group to which people are 100 percent dedicated. Work may be done individually. However, all work is visible to that person's teammates and flows through regular team meetings and tracking systems. This provides each individual with the support and accountability he or she needs to do the work well.

Transparency: The free flow of information is also essential to good work—information about the vision of the product, the viability of the company, and whether we are on track to meet our commitments. Even the emotional state of coworkers is important and should be surfaced. In my experience, you can't have enough information flowing through a system—it is literally the lifeblood of your organization.

Autonomy: In his acclaimed book *Drive: The Surprising Truth about What Motivates Us*, Daniel Pink points out that self-direction is a primary driver for human engagement. Our systems need to support our people in having autonomy over how they do their work, within the agreed-upon constraints of quality and interoperability, of course. If possible, people should also be granted autonomy over what they work on and when they work on it. If you think this sounds crazy, read up on the incredible work done on Results-Only Work Environments (ROWEs).

Managerial Behavior and Leadership

As the saying goes, "the fish rots from the head," and this is particularly true of process changes within our organizations. The tone set by leadership is an important indicator of whether the organization will revert to familiar dysfunction when the going gets tough—as it always does—or lean into the discomfort and learn—learning being one of the most important skills any organization can develop.

As leaders it's important that we set vision, remove obstacles, and develop the stance of a servant leader. We need to look at our teams and honestly ask what they need and how we can help, and then go help.

It's About Culture

Processes come and go and should remain secondary to the culture they help create. Ultimately, Agile thinking is a structured and formal way to create a culture of safety where collaboration, cooperation, and innovation can take root. And if we as managers and leaders are to create the kind of organizations that can weather turbulent markets and create a better world, this must be our goal.

In this chapter we'll explore some of the ways you can begin to change what you do and how you do it. You can start today by organizing in teams, providing clear vision, and getting out of the way to let your people learn. This is how we can create the kind of business that attracts top talent and inspires them to achieve great things.

Agile Managers
By Ann Konkler

Once upon a time, I was an IT manager charged with spreading Agile practices in a traditional, Fortune 500 company. I quickly recognized that if we really wanted to get the most out of Agile, most of us would need to shift the way we thought about not only our engineering practices but also our leadership and management. I spoke with a vice president on my steering committee, and shared that we needed to seriously rethink our behaviors, analytics, and expectations for our teams.

His response: "I've been doing this for 25 years and have no reason to change now. I must be doing something right because I'm a VP [and you're not]."

Nearly 10 years later, those words still sadden me. I knew then and there that I would do whatever it took to stay out of his part of the organization. And though I've not kept up with his career, I don't imagine he's done very well. In my experience, people and organizations that fail to learn are destined to fail.

Many of us would like to rely on "proven best practice" to get us through tough situations. Unfortunately, the complexities of most situations we face don't lend themselves to simple answers. But take courage. While staying open to learning may seem hard and even painful at first, over the years I've found my willingness to embrace this mindset has actually made my teams stronger and my life easier.

Agile Managers Learn

To be Agile is to be adaptable. To adapt, we must first learn. Learning is not just about gathering knowledge; it requires applying that knowledge in a way that moves us closer to our goals.

Many equate becoming an Agile organization with becoming a learning organization as described by Peter Senge in *The Fifth Discipline*: "... where people continually expand their capacity to create the results they truly desire, where new and expansive patterns of thinking are nurtured, where collective aspiration is set free, and where people are continually learning to see the whole together."

The job of an Agile manager—or a leader of any title—is to foster learning and create an organization that grows and adapts.

In some organizations, an Agile manager may adopt responsibilities that aren't explicitly listed in classic Agile descriptions, such as those for a ScrumMaster or Product Owner. Managers may work alongside their teams to help communicate with external stakeholders, negotiate contracts, manage budgets and the like. These managers who fill in operational gaps are appreciated. However, it's the managers who are focused on clearing the way for teams to continually deliver value, as well as creating and maintaining an environment where people can do their best work, who are really worth their weight in gold.

Agile Managers Clear the Way

> *While all people have the capacity to learn, the structures in which they have to function are often not conducive to reflection and engagement.*
> —Mark K. Miller, from *Peter Senge and the Learning Organization*

Managers are often in a unique position to create an environment conducive to learning for their teams. Every manager in any organization has a set of levers at his or her disposal to influence such an environment. Given one's particular sphere of influence and organizational power, specific levers may vary from manager to manager. However, we can draw on the work of Dr. Glenda Eoyang, an expert in the field of human system dynamics (and what is an organization if not a complex human system?) who describes three categories of factors that can be altered to influence how a team will work:

- Containers, or boundaries. There are physical containers such as where people sit, organizational containers like org charts and role descriptions, psychological containers such as personal identities and relationships, or even conceptual containers like shared goals
- Differences. Diversity of skills, traits, personalities
- Exchanges. How information flows through the organization and how people interact with one another

Speaking to members of the Agile community, *Secrets of Great Management* author Esther Derby made clear that managers need to get out of the business of checking off tasks. Instead, we should be thinking about how we can serve our customers, our business, and our community; only then do we enable the power behind self-organizing teams and create the environment for higher levels of performance. Focusing on containers, differences, and exchanges helps us to do that.

One of the Agile Manifesto principles states: "The best architectures, requirements, and designs emerge from self-organizing teams." But why is this so important? This principle recognizes the scientifically proven power of "the smart swarm"—described by Peter Miller in his book of the same name as a group of individuals who respond to one another and to their environment in ways that give them power, as a group, to cope with uncertainty, complexity, and change. Coping with uncertainty, complexity, and change? That's exactly what Agile is all about.

Self-organization does not eliminate the need for strong leaders and managers. By adjusting containers, dampening or amplifying differences, and altering exchanges, Agile managers can have a tremendous influence on the way a team organizes around work to be done or a problem to solve. They can unleash a smart swarm.

And yet in spite of these factors' powerful influence, they don't actually determine the outcomes. Only people can do that.

Agile Managers Support People

A manager's job is to support their people as they do their best work. Even in less-than-stellar times, Agile managers hold close this thought expressed eloquently by Norman Kerth in his book *Project Retrospectives* :

"Regardless of what we discover, we understand and truly believe that everyone did the best job he or she could, given what was known at the time, his or her skills and abilities, the resources available, and the situation at hand."

Like W. Edwards Deming, Agile managers believe "the aim of leadership is not merely to find and record failures of men, but to remove the causes of failure." A strong leader focuses on working the system, not the people.

Agile managers pay attention to what science has known for decades: that engaged, motivated people drive results. As Dan Pink notes in his book *Drive* (a must-read for any manager), people are primarily motivated by three things:

- Mastery: our urge to make progress and get better at what we do
- Autonomy: our desire to be self-directed
- Purpose: our yearning to contribute and to be part of something larger than ourselves

Most agree that a manager must focus on business results. An Agile manager, however, knows that when you create an environment where people are motivated, they thrive. And when people thrive, that's when the bottom line really improves by orders of great magnitude.

Agile Managers Model Agile

A number of Agile/Lean values and principles apply specifically to managers:

- Eliminate waste
- Feedback

- See the whole
- Openness
- Communication
- Empower the team
- Respect
- Courage
- Simplicity
- Focus
- Amplify learning

Agile managers understand where their teams are today while keeping an eye out for the next step in their organization's Agile journey. Being Agile means learning from where we are and where we've been so that the future is that much better. Complacency won't do. Through it all, Agile managers demonstrate by their actions—what they do, say, reward, and recognize—that they value learning and the type of environment that it takes to learn safely.

Conclusion

Agile management is not a new style. It's about taking what we have learned about what's true, letting go of the past (in some cases), and rolling up our sleeves to do the hard work to put all this knowledge into action.

Are you ready?

The Agile Project Manager
By Julie Chickering

I am a risk taker—before becoming a mother I used to regularly jump out of airplanes—and when I first started my Agile journey on a pilot project in 2003 it felt like a risky and "mystical" thing.

As a Project and Program Manager, I had a lot of questions. Was this just the process of the month? If it failed would I still have a job? If I became an awesome ScrumMaster would I work myself out of a job? Others had questions too and were afraid they would have to leave the comfort of their cube and sit in a team room.

As we piloted, we discovered issues and concerns that didn't fit nicely within the constraints of our organization's current structure. There was a lack of coaching and understanding at all levels of what it meant to be Agile. As the pilot teams grew into an Agile pilot program, it began to feel as though there was judgment within the organization as to who could or couldn't become Agile.

Yes, You'll Still Have a Job

As Agile has become more popular, people are beginning to look at Agile transformations differently. As a coach, I have helped hundreds of people on their Agile journey through team launches, program launches, and across organizations and individual coaching in various roles. I believe there is an excitement growing about Agile at every level. However, people still need assurance that they will be supported and valued along their journey, that they will still have a job.

My hope is that not only will they still have a job, but a job they love! As my fellow coach Isaac Montgomery says, "Agile doesn't want your job, Agile needs everybody." And that includes Project Managers.

Managing a Self-Managed System

The Scrum framework is simple by design. A well-tuned Scrum team is self-organizing, self-managing, and can predictably deliver working product over time at a sustainable pace. Most new teams think this sounds too good to be true, as they are usually asked to improve quality while working at an unsustainable pace.

Given its simple framework, some organizations jump to the conclusion that Agile doesn't need project managers, program managers, delivery managers, directors, PMOs, or other key players. As Agile scales, however, the support system of the Scrum teams also needs to scale. And we need experienced people helping to coordinate and enable the smooth flow of work to deliver high-value, high-quality products. There really is a place for everyone to contribute.

Who Can Be Agile?

The question isn't who can and can't be Agile. Everyone can. The real question is: What I can do to enable the Agile journey within our organizations and the community?

I don't jump out of airplanes anymore, but I do get on airplanes every week to incrementally shift conversations with people and organizations.

Agile Organizations—Daring Greatly

By Jean Tabaka

"... there is no effort without error and shortcoming; but who does actually strive to do the deeds; who knows great enthusiasms, the great devotions; who spends himself in a worthy cause; who at the best knows in the end the triumph of high achievement, and who at the worst, if he fails, at least fails while daring greatly ..."

—Theodore Roosevelt, April 23, 1910

Dr. Brené Brown opens her bestselling book *Daring Greatly* with this quote by Theodore Roosevelt. Through it, we see how powerful one person can be when he or she chooses to "dare greatly." But what does this mean for an organization? How does this apply to Agile? And what can we do now to become organizations that truly dare greatly?

Agile transformations request a lot from us: they ask that we stick our toe in unfamiliar organizational waters and step outside our comfort zone. This requires some pretty significant daring on our part and a lot of organizational vulnerability. But with that daring and vulnerability come great gifts and the potential to create sustainable and transformative Agile change that goes beyond mere adoption.

Daring greatly and acting through vulnerability require courage. Think about an organization steeped in practices of detailed, long-term plans. While this planning may seem to provide the organization with a sense of security and direction, that isn't always the case. What does it look like to act courageously in such an environment? How does it feel to invite change despite our fears?

Instead of holding on to long-term plans, we seek opportunities for change. We recognize that as we welcome change we also welcome growth.

Cultivate a Culture of Vulnerability

"Failure is not an option." "You better be right." "I'm trusting you; don't screw up." Does any of this sound familiar? Each of those statements is a prime example of organizational invulnerability.

Daring greatly requires that we cultivate vulnerability—that we open up and run toward difficult things—knowing that our work may be harder and that we may eventually falter.

This is hard enough to think about as an individual, let alone from an organizational point of view. To be vulnerable, a company must be prepared to take bold risks, even if it means potentially appearing too exposed. When we let down walls of invulnerability, we show tremendous courage and create opportunities for continuous learning. And in these deep breaths of vulnerability, the seeds of an Agile adoption grow to become true Agile transformation.

Eliminate Shame, Comparison, and Disengagement

Think about how your organization sets goals and what the ramifications are for not achieving them. Does your organization have a culture of empathy or shame? Are team members meant to feel empowered by their learning or ashamed by their failure? If it's the former, you're on the right path in daring greatly to be Agile. If it's the latter, your Agile adoption will most likely fail.

Shame is corrosive. Comparison demoralizes. And when employees experience these things, they disengage. In such a toxic culture, the organization has ensured that no team will act courageously or cultivate its own vulnerability. Employees won't step forward with an eye toward innovation and growth; they will hold back for fear of being perceived as failures. Teams will set low standards, adopt inattention to results, and discourage accountability.

To be truly transformative, our organizations must not only act courageously and cultivate vulnerability, they must eliminate shame. Despite historically popular motivational tactics, shame is diametrically opposed to long-term team resilience and employee engagement. We eliminate shame within our organizations by embracing empathy, cultivating compassion, and nurturing understanding. Successful Agile transformations can only thrive in organizations that are free from shame. By eliminating shame, teams turn small failures into fast-learning opportunities.

Daring greatly is both an individual and organizational skill. Such daring requires courage, vulnerability, and the elimination of shame, comparison, and disengagement. If you feel your organization is ready for a healthy Agile transformation, dare greatly and help create a culture that embodies a spirit of innovation and learning.

Create Your Own Reality

By Niki Kohari

"The old adage 'People are your most important asset' is wrong. People are not your most important asset. The right people are."
—Jim Collins, author of *Good to Great*

We understand that a truly great company starts with the right people. And that means that as an organization we value people who genuinely care about their work and who are motivated to realize their full potential. We select people who continually reflect on what really matters to them, because at Rally we hire people, not positions. We understand that the best people for our company are those who seek roles where they can learn, grow, and challenge themselves in new ways.

Because we want to be part of an employee's journey and not just the destination, Rally was founded on the core value of "create your own reality." In other words, we give everyone the latitude to pursue their unique career path by encouraging each person to explore opportunities that align personal values with the goals of the organization. This requires us to foster an environment where employees must regularly assess where they are and where they want to be in the future. It also requires us to be open and transparent about the goals of the organization so that Rally's direction is visible to every employee at the company.

We consider "create your own reality" an essential piece of our organization not only because it allows employees to pursue their passions, but also because it is necessary for organizational success.

To be an Agile company, we have to monitor the environment and adapt to stay ahead of the competition. As with every business, we are constantly confronted with new challenges. But unlike most businesses, our approach to finding a solution is unique. We don't ask how; we ask who. Who should be responsible for leading the development of a solution?

We believe that to achieve the best results, we must leverage the talents and passions of our people. Experience has shown us that our team members do their best work when they receive a sense of personal fulfillment from their accomplishments.

While the definition of "create your own reality" is shared among everyone at Rally, each employee is able to enact this value in a way that matches his or her personal goals and aspirations. This means that, as a company, we often create new roles and job titles, allow individuals to move laterally into an open position on a new team or in a different department, or expand current job descriptions so that people can take on new responsibilities.

If you walk the halls of Rally, you'll meet lots of people who have successfully created their own reality. While there are many stories that illustrate this value, here are two great examples:

Bob Cotton was hired as the Engineering Manager about eight years ago, heading up a team of seven developers and testers. About a year after joining the company, he felt compelled to spend more time pursuing his passion for test automation, and so created a new role where he could work on it full time. As Rally continued to grow, it became obvious that more time needed to be dedicated to load and performance testing, so Bob moved into a role where he was the primary developer of the Rally Usage and Statistics Tracker (RUST). After heading up development there for four years, he took his sabbatical. (Each employee who works at Rally for over seven years is able to take six weeks off to pursue other passions.) This was the perfect time to reflect again on what he wanted to pursue next at Rally. When he came back, he transitioned into a new role at Rally,

Principal Engineer, where he paves the way for new technology adoption in our products. In eight years, Bob has been able to create his own reality three times.

Upon graduation, Stephanie Tanner was hired at Rally as a software engineer. While she strongly considered going to graduate school, she opted to see what the job market had to offer. Not long after joining the company, she expressed an interest in user experience. Because she wanted to develop expertise in this area, she was encouraged to seek mentorship from our UX gurus. She started off devoting five hours a week to user experience work, everything from reading and research to interviewing customers and talking with our internal coaches about customer problems. Stephanie now spends about 40 percent of her time working with this team and hopes to move into a full-time role soon. She was able to explore her passion on the job rather than going to school to learn about it.

While Rally may be considered unique for having this core value, anyone can pursue a career path that makes them happy and fulfilled; all you need to do is understand your personal "hedgehog." Though this concept may sound strange, the idea came from the parable of the cunning fox and the simple hedgehog, which business consultant and author Jim Collins discusses in his book *Good to Great*. In the story, the fox continually comes up with new ways to eat the hedgehog, but the hedgehog always wins because of his ability to roll up into a ball of sharp spikes. The hedgehog does this one thing and does it well. Your personal "hedgehog" is the simple guiding principle that drives you toward the intersection of what you enjoy doing, what you were made to do, and what you can make a living doing.

According to Collins you can do a simple exercise to find your hedgehog. All you need are three sheets of paper and the advice of a few trusted friends or colleagues. On the first sheet of paper, answer the question: What am I most passionate about? On the second sheet of paper, answer this: What was I born to do? On the third sheet of paper, list out answers to the last question: What can I actually make a living doing? You should do these independently and then ask others for advice on a job that might overlap aspects of all three groups. When you find that overlap, you should create a plan to make that role your reality.

Everyone Be Agile:
Nine Extraordinary Benefits
Nondevelopment Departments Enjoy
By Jessica Kahn

While serving as part of an Agile marketing team for the last four years, I've seen firsthand the tremendous benefits Agile can provide to practically every department, ranging from accounting to procurement to sales operations. The Agile mindset focuses every organizational function on value creation, fundamentally improving the quality of output, shrinking time to delivery, and significantly improving day-to-day collaboration and quality of work life.

Here are nine benefits and their associated Agile practices that will change the way your organization will work for the better.

Agile Practice: Obsessive Focus on Delivering Value
Benefit: The whole organization moves faster

Value delivery is not just for developers! From human resources' recruitment programs to the IT help desk, in an Agile organization each team looks for faster ways to deliver value to their stakeholders. Waiting a long time for the perfect outcome doesn't fly. Instead, you'll see frequent, helpful, valuable output. For example, marketing might deliver the first round of an evaluation guide for the sales team to use, knowing that a more complete version will appear a few weeks later.

Agile Practice: The Ritual of Appreciations
Benefit: Excellent working relationships

Senior Agile Fellow Jean Tabaka brought the ritual of Appreciations to Rally. In Jean's words: "I learned about the practice from Esther Derby, largely about the importance of the language. You say the person's name, then, 'I appreciate you for ...' And that recipient acknowledges the appreciation by simply saying, 'Thank you.' The recipient's acceptance of that compliment via this simple response is as important as the appreciation itself."

Expect warmer relationships among colleagues and in meetings that start with grateful acknowledgment and acceptance of each other's helpful work. This ritual builds camaraderie and promotes better working relationships among colleagues.

Agile Practice: The Daily Standup
Benefit: Better team coordination

In the Agile environment, every team conducts daily standup meetings. These status updates can prevent confusion or duplication of work by providing useful, real-time information. As the team grows, the standups may evolve and shift. That's okay. You'll discover different cadences and new ways to communicate more effectively as the organization develops.

Agile Practice: Assigning a Product Owner, Delivery Team, and ScrumMaster
Benefit: Clearer roles and responsibilities

These roles are crucial to the Agile process. The product owner (or owners) represents the stakeholders and serves as the voice of the customer. The delivery team performs the work. And the Scrum Master removes impediments and helps keep the team's work flowing. This process ensures that the customer is kept front and center while also providing a harmonious working environment for the team.

Agile Practice: The Iteration Demo
Benefit: Delighted and involved customers and stakeholders

With customers involved early in the process, you are able to maximize their delight much earlier in the process. The Iteration Demo brings customers (or internal stakeholders) in from the start with the involvement and buy-in that comes from seeing the journey unfold. This practice prevents waste and helps focus the team.

Agile Practice: Planning with Kanban Boards
Benefit: Less wasted work

Kanban boards help organize the entire process. Almost every department or cross-functional project team should plan and track projects using this useful tool. Frequent Kanban board check-ins keep major campaigns on track and enable the delivery team to quickly identify what must happen to keep work flowing. The process also rapidly homes in on blockages when they occur.

Agile Practice: Retrospect
Benefit: Better results faster

Since Agile is so focused on regularly assessing the progression of projects and improving the process, you can expect to see better, more effective results. Frequent Retrospective meetings allow teams to identify what is and isn't working so they may plan for a better experience in the future. You may wish to order several copies of Eric Ries's book *The Lean Startup*, which suggests methods for successful product launches.

Agile Practice: Collaboration
Benefit: Early problem solving

Agile organizations don't appreciate the silent and stealthy worker who pulls heroics. They value transparency, humility, and the ability to ask for help early in a project. Through collaboration, Agile organizations seek to find the best outcome for a problem before precious time and money are wasted. And they expect their fellow team members to share this value.

Agile Practice: People over Processes

Benefit: More satisfied employees and better retention

Ultimately, Agile puts the importance on people. When all departments embrace Agile, they give their people the trust, respect, and empowerment needed to be productive, happy employees who can manage their personal and professional obligations. Agile organizations create more satisfied employees, because they are valued as people who have full lives that require flexibility to balance their work and life responsibilities. Satisfied employees who feel respected as people become more loyal to the organization, leading to higher retention rates, better organizational knowledge, and a massive competitive advantage. There is really no better reason to go Agile.

Facilitating the Right Environment
By Mark Kilby

One of the keys to successful Agile coaching is being able to bring the "collaborative environment" to an organization. This begins through the art of facilitation—the process of guiding a group through conversation, constructive conflict, and consensus to achieve an objective. No matter where an Agile coach is serving, she brings to the table a few paramount skills.

An experienced Agile coach creates a safe environment by allowing all voices in the room to be heard. That means giving the extroverts the chance to speak while allowing the introverts to ponder the conversations ... and then speak. In a well-facilitated conversation, you will notice that everyone participates.

An experienced Agile coach allows flexibility, but always with constraints. If the group has not gone through the process of forming, storming, and norming, the Agile coach can guide the group members through this crucial procedure "in the moment." By setting working agreements for the current conversation and letting the group explore the topics and options at hand, the coach will work with the group members to achieve their goal together.

An experienced Agile coach ensures an outcome. By the end of every meeting, participants will always take some action "back to the desk" that they can live with and truly support.

An experienced coach values serving over success. For instance, if the team is still storming or norming, the coach may focus on getting team members to "perform" together over trying to achieve the objective of the meeting. By guiding team members on how to focus together, the coach will help build a collaborative environment that allows the team to achieve all future goals with greater speed and quality.

Why Coaching?

By Mark Kilby

When people ask me why they need an Agile coach, I like to offer a simple explanation: learning Agile is similar to learning to ride a bicycle. Sure, you can do it on your own, but that is often a difficult and painful process full of risks that waste precious time and drain valuable resources. Working with a coach alleviates that pain while providing the kind of safe space that fosters true growth and leads to swift and steady results. In short, by guiding your organization through a series of the most effective and efficient experiences, the Agile coach can reduce the scrapes and bruises that come from learning something new, and can maximize the overall results.

What is an Agile coach?

Put simply, an Agile coach is a trained professional who knows how to implement Agile techniques and disciplines across a variety of industries and circumstances. A skilled coach will always have experience in at least two or more of the most commonly used approaches: Scrum, Extreme Programming, and Kanban. Using a deep understanding of the process, the coach specializes in determining which framework will be the best fit for the organization.

But an Agile coach can only do so much.

Agile adoption involves developing a variety of skills and disciplines, and learning new ways to react. But even more critically, it requires creating the right kind of environment—a specialty of Agile coaches.

It's important to remember that Agile adoption can impact the entire organization. By working with the client to develop servant leaders, guide managers, and manage consequences and results, the Agile coach can create an environment where failing happens fast (and always safely) and where slowing down can actually speed things up.

An Example: Learning to Ride (or: From Wobbling to Pedaling)

From the beginning, I knew this client was headed down a rough road. His company had recently acquired several other companies and merged their technologies to build a "comprehensive solution." But all of the teams were building different parts of the "solution" and they were quickly heading in separate directions. The company was falling behind in the marketplace, the solution was becoming difficult to use (colliding with customer expectations), and loyal customers were questioning if they wanted to stay onboard for the ride.

Originally, the company had decided to try out Scrum—the popular Agile software development method for managing software projects—on its own, but later decided to bring me in as coach. We started with a two-day workshop where we brought together as much of the team as we could in one place. They resisted the expense at first, but ultimately found that having all the "conversations" in one room empowered the participants to make more decisions in a day than they could in three months of endless emails and smaller meetings. They were learning to ride faster and more efficiently *together*.

We talked about where they were trying to go: the product vision. No one on the team seemed to have the same destination, let alone the same roadmap. Through a series of exercises, we discussed what customers and businesses needed and what kind of ride the technology could provide. Together we set a new vision that was audacious but obtainable.

Finally, we started looking at the details of the team members' first milestone. As we discussed the different paths they were exploring, and how Scrum could get them there, they became somber. They realized they couldn't do everything they had planned; they had to make some hard decisions. We went through more exercises and came up with a unified plan that would help them reach their milestone. They were learning to pace themselves for longer and more successful rides.

Since that time, they have had some great rides and a few spectacular crashes. What the team participants learned was to take the time to stop and observe along the way. By taking this time to reflect, they discovered how to go faster and with more control each time. Where are they now? Three years later, they have launched the latest version of their comprehensive solution and are once again a key contender in the market.

Enjoy the Ride
Like organizations themselves, the coaching process comes in all shapes and sizes. Depending on the size and scope of the project, you may need an Agile coach for anywhere from a few months to a couple years. Remember, it's a process. And because one coach may not have knowledge of all the frameworks and skills, it may require more than one coach. In fact, a community of coaches is often the most effective way to get a large group to "ride to success." And that's exactly what it is: a ride.

With the help of a coach, you can ride faster, go farther, and achieve success in ways you never thought possible. In short, a coach can help you create the ride of your life. Enjoy that ride.

Agile in Distributed Environments
By Tamara Nation

The global presence and offshore phenomenon in the IT space have created widely distributed teams that can vary in size and complexity. Regardless of the details of distribution, the challenges and even complaints of distributed teams are similar: they're costly and they tend to face communication challenges. Fortunately, Agile values can guide leaders of distributed teams to success even under the most extreme circumstances.

The first difficult fact you must accept about distributed teams is that they're darn hard to do! The best way to communicate will always be face-to-face, by any measure of effectiveness. Studies indicate that voice-only communication is almost 60 percent less effective than face-to-face. And email, the favored method of communication with our overseas peers, is the least effective method possible. Given that the methods commonly used for distributed collaboration are email and phone calls, this leads to another major challenge.

Distributed teams are more expensive than you think. There is a growing understanding of the true cost of large geographic and time zone differences. The burden of close communication (the only real way to build a great team) can be keenly and prohibitively felt by everyone if the time difference between team locations is more than eight hours. The diminished effectiveness associated with midnight calls and lost sleep is hard to measure. Off-hours for standups and planning meetings maintain the Agile value of collaboration while violating the Agile value of creating a sustainable pace.

The solution is in part the same one Agilists always recommend: bring everyone together for face-to-face collaboration for planning and retrospective meetings. This is the best way to create a team out of a group of distributed individual contributors. If you are the leader of a distributed team, plan for quarterly or more frequent get-togethers for everyone working in your value stream. These meetings should be centered on creating a common vision of the work and steady improvement of the communication processes. There is no shortcut to building a great team; it takes a lot of time and good communication.

In addition to a regular cadence of travel for face-to-face meetings, you should find and experiment with collaborative tools. Most teams struggle with good communication, but luckily there are some fantastic tools available. Video conferencing, virtual development, and collaboration environments are becoming more common and cost effective even for small teams. Researching and learning these tools can be time consuming but they are well worth the effort. The key to using these tools effectively is to have everyone, regardless of their location, use the same method for communication. Once more effective tools are in place, teams can start to talk, share screens, and work with relative ease.

A final solution for distributed teams is to try and avoid the situation altogether. Instead of splitting teams or functional areas, think about distributing entire workstreams to a specific location. What if the India-based test team owned an entire functional area rather than just the testing? What would it look like to create cross-functional teams at each of your locations that enjoyed all the benefits of co-location?

Although distributed teams can create challenges, they can also be highly successful. Over the years, I have observed many distributed teams who excel in their Agile practices. However, it requires a significant investment of time and money to enjoy that kind of success.

The Importance of Space
By Alex Pukinskis

In the 1990s, IBM asked Alistair Cockburn to define its software development process, so he started watching successful project teams. One of the key patterns he saw was a behavior he called "osmotic communication"—these teams were sitting close enough together that people were regularly overhearing relevant information. Cockburn's theory is that the speed of a project is determined by the speed of the information flow between team members.

Your Space Is Defining Your Culture

Where people sit, whom they sit near, whether they're in the same area or the same floor or the same building, the way you've set up your walls, the type of furniture in the room—all of these elements have a deep, fundamental impact on the culture you create and the products you build.

Look at the image of the offices on the following page.

How fast do you think information flows in each of these spaces? What culture do you imagine each one has? Do these people have shared goals or separate responsibilities? Do they talk to each other a lot, or do they tend to work alone? Do they eat lunch together? What kind of products do they produce? Are they well integrated, or do they have clear separation?

Create the right space and you'll find that your culture shifts to drive better business outcomes.

So what layout is the best for maximizing information flow within teams? Here are five layouts that offer very different impacts:

Private Offices can help concentration and reduce distractions, which led Tom DeMarco and Tim Lister to advocate for them in their classic book *Peopleware*. If you're engaged in a tough problem, it's easy to stay focused in this type of space.

But if you're stuck, it's also easy to stay stuck. A closed door makes it hard to ask for help. If you want to chat with someone, you may walk by a glass door, see that they're busy, and decide to move on.

This is a layout optimized for individual productivity, not for maximizing information flow within teams.

Full-size Cubicles often appear in cultures where people would like private offices but they've been deemed too expensive. You have the benefit of some visual privacy, and this will be a bit less noisy than an open floor plan.

But you are still forced to hear every single sound made in the next cube. And cubes cause interruptions. Since you can't see into them, you end up interrupting just by checking if someone is in. Once you're standing there, you might as well ask the question. Plus, people tend to chat over the walls, distracting everyone else.

You've got all of the isolation of a private office, but none of the privacy.

An **Open Layout with Fixed Systems Furniture** is the obvious improvement. Reduce the heights of the cubicles so people can see each other more easily. You can glance over to see if someone's busy. You can easily tell who's around so you don't waste time hunting for people. And you save money by building at higher density—where a 6x6-closed cube feels like a box, a 6x6-open workspace isn't too bad.

But this layout is optimized for completely unfiltered communication. Most of the time, people in this kind of layout are sitting near people doing incompatible work. A salesperson on the phone all day with customers can ruin the concentration for an adjacent engineer. If that engineer complains and is moved to a desk near the lunchroom, the visual and auditory distractions can decimate productivity.

Even if you seat teammates together, the systems furniture itself can be a problem. Many engineers in an Agile environment find it's effective to work together on problems much of the time—like movers carrying a couch, a pair can do heavy lifting more easily than one person struggling alone. But L-shaped corner desks make it impossible to sit side-by-side—they're optimized for one person, sitting alone.

Finally, a fixed layout makes it tough to deal with changes to team sizes. Either you:

1. Leave lots of desks empty so you have room to add people to teams, or
2. Shuffle everyone around when you need to add one person, or
3. Give up on locating teams near each other and stick that extra person in the empty cube near the break room

While the fixed, open layout often seems like an exciting change from full cubes, it's really the worst of both worlds—noisy, little flexibility, and little privacy.

Team Rooms
Modeled after a science lab, a team room is a shared space for a small team of 5 to 10 people. Ideally this room has solid walls, windows, and a door that closes.

If the team is working toward a single, shared goal, this layout optimizes for team productivity. The team members own the space and move furniture around as they choose, so there's a strong sense of team identity. The walls provide plenty of space to hang whiteboards for collaborative work.

When there's a clear, shared goal, the energy that you feel when you walk into a room like this is palpable. And indeed, outsiders hesitate at the door, knowing that if they come in and interrupt, it had better be important and relevant.

Open, Movable Layout
The last four layouts have one thing in common: they're hard to change. Even the "flexible" systems furniture can cost thousands to move and rewire for a simple adjustment. So people are more likely to suffer through a layout that isn't working. Over time, the lack of flexibility makes it hard to keep teams together.

In an open, movable layout, engineers drag their tables together when they're working on a shared project. Power and network drop from the ceiling. When someone new joins a team, it's easy to drag over another table and pull up a chair. Easily movable partitions create auditory and visual privacy exactly where it's needed, and the teams can move them when their needs change.

It's common to see this layout in startup companies, where there simply isn't enough money to build out an expensive, fixed layout. Without movable partitions this kind of space gets really noisy as you exceed 30 people. At Rally, we've invested in 8-foot-high, 8-inch-thick T-walls on heavy casters with whiteboards. Teams that need more privacy use these as sound buffers and to create a sense of personal space. Unlike a team room, you can adjust the size of your area in an afternoon, without getting any permission except from the team next to you.

We find that about every three months a team needs a change that necessitates an adjustment from three to four other teams around them. Team members take an hour or two to move tables and walls, plug back into the power and network grid, and are up and running again.

This layout has a hidden benefit: If people can arrange it exactly the way they want, they often voluntarily choose a layout that has a higher density (more people per square foot), which reduces costs.

Leveraging the Power of Space at Your Organization

Space can have a huge impact on your success and the speed of your projects. Chances are your layout is causing your projects to take a lot longer than necessary.

So how do you get started creating something better? You don't have to do it all at once. Try putting one team in a good-sized, dedicated team room and letting its members focus on a project. As they learn about what's working, give them the resources they ask for to experiment with the space. They'll show you where you need to go.

Co-located Teams

By Alex Pukinskis

Considering co-location probably sounds crazy if your organization is globally distributed. In today's hyper-connected world, spreading teams across multiple time zones is the norm for many companies. The truth is having a distributed organization may be your reality, but whether you use distributed teams is a choice.

While co-location is not a prerequisite for being Agile, there are many benefits to bringing people together face-to-face. At Rally we have engineering locations in multiple time zones, but we work hard to make sure that teams are sitting together in one location whenever possible. We've found this easier to do than you might think.

It does require a different perspective on staffing: we try to keep teams together over multiple projects. If you're used to teams that have members around the world, this probably seems like a tough change. And it can be. But the gains you experience in productivity and the risk reduction you achieve with more predictability and fewer wrong turns may make it well worth the trouble.

If you're still temporarily stuck with teams that are distributed, expect constant communication challenges. While these challenges can be minimized, they unfortunately will probably never be entirely eliminated.

You may notice your team trying to compensate for the communication costs by asking for technical solutions like videoconferencing hardware or headsets, or to travel for planning meetings. While these things can seem expensive, the cash cost pales in comparison to the delays associated with poor communication.

Agile teams tend to know exactly what's slowing them down, and they raise this knowledge in daily standup meetings and retrospectives. Visibility into these impediments is gold when trying to move forward. In the end, though, the cheapest and most effective way to maximize your throughput is to staff teams with people who are in the same physical location.

Technology may connect the world, but face-to-face communication is still the best way to connect your team.

Sustainable Pace

By Ken Clyne

Among Agile adopters, it's a common belief that Agile processes promote sustainable development and that sponsors, developers, and users should be able to maintain a constant pace indefinitely. But what kind of pace is sustainable? And how do we develop processes that allow our teams to do good work at a constant pace—indefinitely?

When I think of sustainable pace I always recall the episode of *I Love Lucy* where Lucy gets a job at a candy factory. Her only task is to wrap chocolates that arrive on a conveyor belt. As the rate of arrival increases, quality suffers with hilarious results. Although this episode aired 60 years ago, it is as funny today as it was then—despite the fact we all know the punch line.

Regardless of whether we are working on a Scrum team or in a chocolate factory, when we take on too many things at one time, quality suffers. We all know this, yet, despite the best efforts of Stephen Covey and others to educate us, we continue to multitask, change priorities, and work our most valued contributors to the point of exhaustion.

So why do we continue to make the same mistake? Why do people stay so busy and why do they seem to be the most productive in the organization? There are two levers at work here:

1. We want the best people working on the highest priorities, and we want to get as much out of them as we can.

2. Our best people often encourage this, enjoying the sense of urgency, the feeling of job security, and personal value they get from being "indispensable" and overextended.

But most of all, this culture persists because our leaders—the people many look up to and strive to emulate—got where they are through their own superhero efforts. These are the people who have made a difference. How do we change this pervasive culture and present our case to those who have benefitted the most from it? The answer may lie not in a social argument but an economic one.

Don Reinersten, author of *The Principles of Product Development Flow*, says, "Perhaps the single most important weakness of the current orthodoxy is its failure to correctly quantify economics. When done correctly, an economic framework will shine a bright light into all the dark corners of product development."

What bright lights can we shine on our problem of sustainable pace?

Most important, we must start measuring the work product, not the worker. Once we acknowledge this and understand that the single most important factor that affects queue size is capacity utilization, we have established an economic argument for establishing sustainable pace—one that will even resonate with senior management.

Audio, Video, and Virtual Team Realities
By Mark Kilby

When taking part in an Agile transformation, I'm often asked by clients which technology is the best. My typical answer is "none of them." The clients are asking the wrong question.

While virtual teams define our current work reality, there's a common misunderstanding that just applying multiple technologies will make these teams effective. As stated in the Agile Manifesto, individuals and interactions should carry more weight than processes and tools. No single tool will replace the rich ambient information within a co-located space or the camaraderie of a co-located team. Why then are some virtual teams as successful as co-located teams? In my experience, a couple of factors come into play.

They Trust Each Other
Team members have either met each other face-to-face at multiple events or have had opportunities to get to know each other through online channels. They understand and often share their team members' history, values, and professional goals. Provide the opportunity for the members of your virtual team to learn about each other and self-align.

They Stay Connected
In a traditional co-located team, you typically find a more diversified level of daily interaction. On desks, team members see the pictures of family and friends, as well as project progress charts. They notice when a team member comes into the office energized or exhausted. They understand each

other's work-life balance from multiple cues, and understand when to ask for or offer help.

You can create this same sort of intimacy by providing technologies for team members to connect through chat, video in meetings (and throughout the day), and a place to share a bit about their life outside of work. This helps everyone get a more well-rounded understanding of the team.

They Keep the Band Together (as Long as They Still Play Well)

Often virtual teams are dismantled at the end of the project or phase, which means they must re-form and reconnect on a new project—an expensive startup process. The teams that are the most successful usually include some members who have known each other for years or more and who look for new opportunities to work together.

Keeping a successful virtual team together increases the chance that any project it takes on will also be successful. Successful virtual teams also tend to find ways of bringing in new members quickly by constantly renewing the team's shared goals.

Virtual teams are a reality in our current business environment. But while the teams might be virtual, the people behind them require the same things as anyone on any team. Experiment with what works, and do your best to help teams develop a set of virtual tools that allow them to interact with complexity and nuance. Your productivity depends on it.

Social Contracts

By Ryan Martens

One way to think about an Agile transformation is as a giant organiza-tional redesign. This view can scare people because it creates a series of unknowns and makes them question everything, from their value to their purpose. If left unchecked, this kind of anxiety results in FUD (Fear, Uncertainty, and Doubt).

If an Agile transformation is well managed, everyone gets brought into the continuous-improvement effort to make his or her life, role, customers, and co-workers happier. However, in a large transformation, some roles will be redesigned or completely eliminated.

Thanks to 10 years of successful Agile transformations, these organizational tendencies are well documented. As a leader, your job is to beat the FUD and get everyone pulling together for a better future. The only way I have seen this done effectively is through a social contract.

Quite simply, a social contract is the agreement you make with your employees to support them during the journey to Agile—no matter the outcome.

Luckily, I got to work with Cutter Consortium director Israel Gat from 2004 to 2006 as a customer. During the Agile transformation at BMC Software, Israel masterfully leveraged a social contract of employee training to get everyone on board.

In Israel's case, his commitment was to the development of the group's skill set—even if that meant his employees went to another division or company. This was the only thing he could promise given the fact that, as its members started the transition to Agile, the fate of the group's entire division was unknown.

Not all Agile transitions start in an environment as uncertain as that of BMC's Patrol team, but the social contract still remains critical for every organization. As social systems specialist Peter Senge says, "People don't resist change. They resist being changed!" Israel made it clear that the employees would get value out of the transition no matter what their ultimate fate would be. And thanks to that, the Agile transformation was successful.

A Culture of Great Meetings
By Laura Burke

Most meetings suck. And because meetings are an integral part of a company's culture, most company cultures suck as well. At Rally, we believe that if you take the time to build a culture of great meetings you can transform the culture of your company. The steps are simple but, like many things in our Agile toolkit, they are not easy.

To develop a culture of great meetings, you need to follow a few basic practices to engage teams: a solid foundation for the meeting, a few tools, and quick retrospectives. By following these practices, you'll create the kind of engaged teams that can deliver the quality products and services you need to compete.

The Foundation
At the foundation of a great meeting are three key elements: a purpose, an agenda, and consensus.

How many times have you been to a meeting and not understood why you were there? The next time you're setting up a meeting, be sure to remember what it is you're trying to accomplish by getting the group together. Once the purpose is identified, it will help you understand who should be invited, what materials need to be available, and how long the meeting should last. Post the purpose before and during the meeting. When a purpose is made visible, it helps keep the team on track.

Once the purpose has been identified, reflect on the questions you need answered to move forward. From there, you can build a meaningful agenda.

When the meeting starts, check in with the group to confirm that the proposed purpose and agenda meet the participants' needs. This is called building consensus. When people agree on what needs to be accomplished, it's easier for them to engage.

Tools
A few tools will keep you on track.

Use sticky notes or a shared online space (like a Google Doc) to record and quickly prioritize the key elements of the discussion.

Use a timer to keep things moving. Ask the members of the group how much time they want to devote to a particular topic, then use the timer to stick to that schedule. I've often seen groups engage in very interesting conversations that are irrelevant to the meeting's purpose (again, it helps to have the purpose visible). A timer gives the group ownership of how long a discussion should and will last.

A "parking lot"—a place on a whiteboard or flip chart to capture "interesting and important topics" that aren't relevant to the immediate conversation—is critical for making sure that those topics aren't neglected later on. Simply ask: "Can this be put in the parking lot to be discussed later?" If the subject merits further discussion, note it on a sticky and make sure you revisit it before the meeting's close.

Retrospect
Check in at the end of the meeting with a quick retrospective. Ask your team what worked well and what could be done better next time. No matter how thorough the prep for a meeting is, there is always room to improve. It's important to incorporate the group's feedback into your next meeting.

The fact of the matter is, you must have great meetings to become successful at Agile. As you improve your meetings, you will more effectively engage your team and enable your Agile adoption. The process may feel uncomfortable at first, and you may get resistance, but in the end you'll improve both your meetings and your company's culture.

Servant Leadership
By Rachel Weston Rowell

Servant Leadership is a concept proposed by Robert K. Greenleaf in 1970. As Greenleaf described them, Servant Leaders are born out of a desire to serve, which creates an aspiration to lead. It is one extreme on a continuum of leadership types that range from Servant Leaders to those who follow a "Leader First" approach. While most people fall somewhere in the middle, in Agile organizations we see greater success with those leaders who identify with the Servant Leader archetype.

How can you tell if you are a Servant Leader?

Leaders who manifest servant leadership exhibit two behaviors:

- Leading by serving
- Serving by leading

Leading by serving means you create a work environment in which each person is valued and team members' success, happiness, and growth are paramount concerns. You recognize that enriched and satisfied people contribute excellent results to the organization, so you highly value helping each individual achieve. In other words, you are leading the team by *serving* the team.

Serving by leading means you are modeling the behaviors and actions that will guide the team members in their own work so they can contribute their best to the team and organization. You hold the vision for the team and demonstrate excellent results through your actions. Here, you are serving the team by *leading* the team.

Jim Collins has written extensively about "Level 5 Leaders" and how they are key to turning organizations from good companies into great companies. He describes a behavior he calls "the window and the mirror," in which these leaders will assign all accolades for success to those around them (looking through a window) and take responsibility for failure on themselves (looking in a mirror). This is a classic example of Servant Leadership in action, and his examples are testaments to the value of this type of leadership.

Trusting in Conflict
By Mark Kilby

Constructive conflict is critical to the success of a high-performing team. However, without the right foundation, constructive conflict around ideas can quickly fall into destructive conflict based on emotions. In order for team members to move from storming to performing, they must first build a foundation of trust.

High-performing teams need constructive conflict to explore alternative solutions to a problem their members are trying to solve together. To reach the best solution, each team member must provide different perspectives based on his or her experience. For success in implementing the idea together, everyone on the team must also agree on the solution. They all should be able to say, "I can live with that and support it."

Most teams typically misunderstand conflict. Why? We struggle to distinguish between a personal threat and someone having a better idea. When we take it personally, we tell ourselves stories about the intent of the other person. We retaliate with fight or flight. But in reality, what causes our vision to become cloudy is our reluctance to trust our own viewpoint.

When team members feel as though they are using their individual talents to achieve personal goals aligned with a common goal, the perceived value of both the work and the team increases.

It's only when we build trust in the team first that we may fully accept the idea that conflict can actually allow the team members to work more closely to mutual purpose. Team members who develop this level of trust not only "buy into" the solution but also work together to "fight for" the idea rather than "fight against" each other.

4
Agile Steering

Agile Steering

By Bob Gower

Everyone has a plan 'till they get punched in the mouth.

—Mike Tyson

As a product manager in Silicon Valley, I learned the hard way that I needed to plan for surprises. At first I would manage uncertainty by attempting to overpower it. I would research, plan, challenge assumptions, and then create the perfect, detailed product-requirements document that I thought accounted for everything. Then I'd share it with my team and would inevitably be asked questions to which I had no answer.

And as we went deeper into the project, the changes would get more complex, and I would find myself updating my perfect document again and again. It felt like half my job was just to make sure that developers were working from the right version of the requirements—that is, if I got around to updating the doc at all. Often there were huge discrepancies between the product that finally hit production and the requirements document on file, with many of the changes "documented" only in long email threads and private conversations.

And then I'd release the product only to find that we'd missed the mark, and much of what we built was not what the customer actually wanted. This isn't just a problem; it's an epidemic. Is it any wonder that so much of the software out there is so bad?

Risk

After years of working in product development, I've come to believe that the human psyche is so risk-averse that we would rather do almost anything than sit for even a moment in the discomfort of uncertainty. But the reality is that we are working on large, complex projects in dynamic markets with new technology, and uncertainty just comes with the job.

The secret is to plan for change and plan to learn as we plan our products—to dynamically steer our organizations rather than just aim them and hope for the best. If we build our planning systems well and work in a disciplined way, it becomes relatively easy to answer the three most common questions of our business partners: What am I going to get? When will I get it? How much will it cost? And, we can answer these questions well and still build products that delight our customers and are documented for our auditors, users, and future development teams.

Unfortunately, most businesses prefer to write detailed project plans that mask what they don't know rather than take the time to build flexible and transparent steering processes that encourage collaborative work on creative solutions.

The Five Levels of Planning

In all organizations, planning happens in stages: the company vision gets broken down into a product strategy and roadmap, which in turn gets divided into individual releases. As people coordinate their work, they may break things down even further into iteration goals—assuming they are working in iterations. Each individual or team in turn sits down on a daily basis (at least somewhat deliberately, we hope) to plan what they'll accomplish each day. If this process happens efficiently, each person's daily work is directly linked to the company's overall success. But how often does this actually happen in an efficient manner?

When transmitting electricity on high-voltage lines there is a "line loss," meaning some of the electricity is lost in transmission from power plant to home or business. The same thing often occurs with the vision of a business. There is a loss of focus and purpose as we proceed from vision to daily action. A planning cycle provides that clarity and helps your company run more smoothly, with happier employees and more value for your customers.

The five levels of planning—vision, roadmap, release, iteration, and daily—are not presented as a rigid format. Each organization is different and your planning strategy may have more or fewer distinct phases. But if you develop a set of disciplined practices at each level, you'll begin to build the kind of organization that can create great products quickly and cost-effectively.

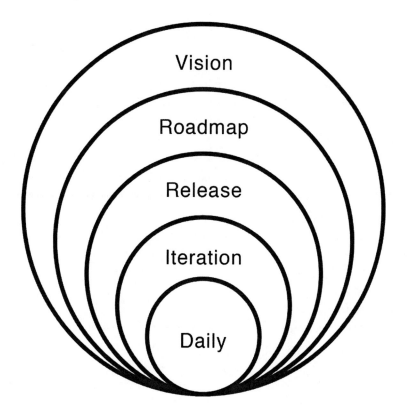

Improving Your Digestion
If you want to improve how your organization plans, the first thing to do is build a system that offers a high degree of visibility and transparency. This allows you to harness the intelligence of your entire organization by crowd-

sourcing solutions and enabling everyone to make better day-to-day individual decisions.

While transparency may seem like a nice thing to have, secrecy in your organization can erode your coworkers' enthusiasm and intelligence. While producing this book at Rally, I regularly shared the content—even the stuff that wasn't "ready"—with the entire organization and each time I learned something that helped me produce a better product. Was it scary? Absolutely! But it was incredibly helpful in making this book the best it could be.

In order to develop this visibility, you'll need a regular cadence of planning meetings at each level of planning. These should be built into your culture and done at regular intervals—even if there's not much to talk about. If you plan only when there's a crisis, you'll have more crises. If you plan habitually and with discipline, you'll only rarely get surprised. This is a good thing.

And the information that flows out of these regular meetings needs to flow in feedback loops that go in both directions. Sure, your release planning needs to inform your iteration planning and daily meetings, but information from daily planning and iteration planning is also vital to your release planning efforts. And the people managing the roadmap need clear information about what's going on at the release level if they're to make the best decisions possible. Feedback circuits are as valuable in organizational design as they are in electrical engineering.

Collaboration

It really all comes down to building a culture and set of systems that allow your people to collaborate at all levels to create the most solid plans they can.

I know you're working in the real world with funding, accounting, and phase gate systems that are based on a very different mindset from what I've presented here. And about now you're probably thinking "this won't work here." If that's the case, I encourage you to review the pieces in this section carefully. We've done our best to address the most common concerns and objections to a more Agile way of doing things. As you read, you'll get a deeper understanding of the topic as well as see a clearer path to applying these principles in your organization.

You may also get a very real idea of the cost associated with not adopting a more dynamic and Agile set of practices. As psychologist Theodore Rubin said, "The problem is not that there are problems. The problem is expecting otherwise and thinking that having problems is a problem."

Agile Portfolio Steering
By Ann Konkler

When I was four years old, I thought driving a car meant turning the key, yanking down on the gear shifter, and stepping on the pedal. I hadn't quite grasped the concept of steering.

Many years later, I learned that good driving requires responding to constant feedback and keeping our eyes and ears open at all times. And I've learned that effectively managing a portfolio is much the same. It involves more than simply deciding we want to go somewhere and then starting the engine. At its core, it's all about steering.

Agile portfolio management (really, steering) is a step toward becoming an Agile enterprise. It's about being nimble and adaptive while paying attention to the fundamentals of running a business. It's about making important decisions based on reliable, real-time information rather than wishful thinking.

At one point, many of us believed these statements to be true:

- A successful project is one that is on time, on budget, and on scope
- Completing project tasks indicates progress toward value delivery
- Moving people from project to project is efficient and effective
- Starting early means finishing early

Okay, maybe we've never really believed any or all of these statements, but others around us have certainly tried to influence us to accept them without challenge. They have defined metrics, instilled processes, built tools, written books, created accredited certification programs, and even built careers based on these common "truths."

Once upon a time, most people also believed the earth was flat. It was accepted as common truth. If we had stayed in one place for our entire life, never looked at pictures taken from space, never read a science textbook, perhaps we too would have accepted it as truth because everyone else around us had. However, examining the evidence and exploring the terrain for ourselves allow us to recognize that a richer existence is possible.

Learning to Drive

Steering a portfolio toward value starts with paying attention to meaningful feedback, what's really true. Given that our portfolios are designed to create a return on investment, we're interested in regularly checking how well we're doing on realizing that return. And so we define a set of metrics that we believe will give us this information, and we start tracking accordingly. The tricky part is in knowing which indicators will give us useful information and which might be distractions that could take us off our intended path.

It can be tempting to put too much emphasis on checking off completed tasks on a project plan; it's easy information to track and easy to ask for. Caution is warranted here. Counting how many turns we've made doesn't necessarily reveal how close we are to our destination. We're much better off focusing on the mileposts along the side of the highway. "Are we there yet?" is actually the best question to ask. In software delivery, or any product development effort, the delivered value matters most.

When we check our indicators is also important. Meaningful feedback is always regular and frequent. It's based on what's happening right now; it isn't delayed or distorted by passing from one source to another.

The right tools for tracking progress can absolutely do wonders for timely feedback. However, when navigating complex and uncertain territory, the most vital feedback usually comes from the passengers in the car—not the tools. Always remember that people know things that will never show up on a dashboard. Invite them to share and to share frequently.

Inviting collaboration and increasing visibility for everyone along for the ride also comes with some surprising side benefits. When we offer cascading context and insight, people closest to the work are better equipped to make critical, yet seemingly small, decisions when the answers matter most. Moreover, when people can see that their work aligns directly to a larger vision—that their work really matters—stand back! You've just cleared the windshield and unleashed an amazing power.

Planning the Trip

Of course, managing a portfolio involves more than just tracking and maintaining alignment. We also need to have a good picture of our organizational capabilities and capacity so that we can make sound decisions about where we should invest and when.

Many organizations attempt to get their arms around this aspect of longer-range planning by asking for upfront effort estimates along with a detailed breakdown of the skills required for each proposed initiative. And then this information is usually mapped to individual people by checking their availability and expertise levels to decide if/when the initiative can be completed in the desired timeframe.

Traditional resource management makes sure that people are kept busy far into the future, striving for as little downtime as possible. It also supports the notion that any initiative with a good business case should be funded and started as soon as a few people can begin work.

Would you start out on a long trip if the only road out of town was clogged with a bunch of cars all heading the same way? How well can you predict your arrival time when stuck in a traffic jam? How about when traffic flows freely?

In the world of portfolio management, it's not unusual for organizations to clog their delivery pipeline by starting as many initiatives as are approved and funded. While hoping to finish early by starting early, the opposite usually occurs. Projects end up running later than expected. And worse, once they get stuck in the jam, people have an even harder time predicting when they will be done than they did in providing the original estimate.

In business, we strive to deliver quickly to maximize our returns. However, focusing only on speed can be misleading and may even slow us down. Predictability can be just as important as speed and perhaps even more so. Reliably understanding when something will finish matters more when we're in the middle of coordinating multiple teams, making trade-off decisions, and trying to hit the market at just the right moment. It may sound surprising, but better predictability and faster delivery come from working on less, not more.

Consider the impact of starting three initiatives at the same time, where implementation requires attention from the same group of people.

If we started all three and asked the team members to divide their attention equally, we will have created a bottleneck and unnecessarily prolonged the delivery time of all but the last initiative. Revenue realization is delayed until the end of the cycle.

The picture changes significantly when we stop starting and start finishing. Opportunities for benefit realization appear much sooner. Productivity dramatically improves.

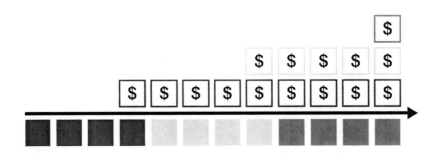

Focus counts at the team level too. Pulling people off mid-project to fight fires or to start another initiative creates a ripple effect of delays. According to a rule of thumb described by Gerald Weinberg in *Quality Software Management*, if I'm working on three separate but concurrent initiatives, then I shouldn't expect any more than 60% of my total available time will be spent on actual work. When teams stay together and focus, however, they find their rhythm and throughput stabilizes.

Granted, there's no guarantee of *maximum* throughput simply because we have persistent and dedicated teams or have limited our work in process. Throughput can be affected by any number of variables in an organization's processes and in the technical environment. However, flowing work through teams, instead of people through projects, eliminates a major source of variability.

Getty Images recently went through a major overhaul in how they think about portfolio planning—creating an initiative and feature roadmap that balances higher business goals against the reality of their organization's capacity and throughput, without spending an inordinate amount of time on up-front estimates. The photo agency appears to have found the planning sweet spot.

In his book *Agile Estimating and Planning*, Mike Cohn describes the sweet spot as the point where just enough effort has been put into estimating, but not so much as to create a false sense of accuracy due to listing out details that we can't possibly know so far in advance of implementation. Cohn writes, "Sometimes spending just a little time thinking about an estimate is just as good or better than spending a lot of time thinking about it."

Recalling a previous work environment, Nina Shoen, PMO Director at Getty Images, describes a situation where there was no room for discovery, no room for responding to market changes, no room for anything to change at all. In Nina's words, "The plans were hilarious."

Start the Journey

Let's face it: a prediction of the future will never be more than a guess until it's history. Any plan you put in place today may be wrong tomorrow. So hurry up, get something sketched out, and steer from there. Keep your eyes open. The view might be a little frightening at first, but with the right feedback on the right cadence, you'll have what you need to avoid a serious collision … and maybe even most of the potholes.

Funding and Accounting in an Agile World

By Brent Barton

How we spend our company's money reflects our strategy. It is a "dollar" representation of our priorities, our values, our goals and our aspirations.
— Jim Lejeal, Rally's Chief Financial Officer

While cost considerations seem absent from many Agile conversations, how we spend money directly aligns to the value we try to deliver.

Value to our customers is both implicit and explicit in our strategic goals. Our prospects and customers communicate their perception of value when they spend their precious dollars on our products and services; and what we value as a company is expressed by what we choose to fund.

Agile methods do not address investment strategies and cost accounting directly. Even though the word "value" is used several times in the Agile Manifesto, the meaning behind what is valuable is not articulated. For example, the first principle says, "Our highest priority is to satisfy the customer through early and continuous delivery of valuable software." This is the only reference that indicates a strategy exists. Cost, in the form of labor, is only implicit because "we value individuals and interactions."

To be successful in business, we need to be able to articulate value in terms of strategies and investments. We must be able to prioritize our work and make trade-off decisions based on how much time and money we have spent compared to the potential returns on these investments. Shorter cycles and smaller increments of completed functionality should give us better intermediate information more quickly, which should increase our ability to make evidence-based trade-offs. Still, traditional funding and accounting methods have gaps when used with Agile practices that promote shorter, smaller increments of completed functionality.

To keep things simple, we'll use a startup example as a way to demonstrate cost accounting—how we have spent our company's money. Through this example we'll discover what value means. Viewed from this small starting place, we can then consider how things work at a larger company and add some perspectives that scale creates.

Know Your Burn Rate

A long time ago, I was in a startup. We were an Internet darling and our stock options were going to be worth a fortune. It was Tuesday morning. Everyone had arrived at the all-hands meeting. By now, we were a bit too large for everyone to meet in our office so we rented a local movie theater. The CEO opened the meeting this way:

We ran out of money as of yesterday and cannot pay your salaries going forward. Yesterday, in the eleventh hour, our next round of funding failed. One of our previous investors may step in and is on-site right now. You may stay this week and risk not getting paid or leave now and we will cut you a check through yesterday ...

This is an all-too-common example of the high-risk world of startups. It is a race to get to revenue and then profitability, or you must find more funding, or the company dies. In this environment, your focus is on how much cash you have on hand and how fast you're burning through it.

As an example, let's say that we have $500,000 to invest in the development of a new software product, and we determine that we should hire five people who each have a total annual cost of $100,000 (see tables on following page). To keep things simple, I've cut from this example fixed operational costs, like rent and server space, and variable costs like payroll taxes and benefits.

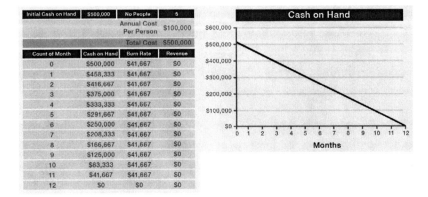

Initial Cash on Hand	$500,000	No People	5
		Annual Cost Per Person	$100,000
		Total Cost	$500,000
Count of Month	Cash on Hand	Burn Rate	Revenue
0	$500,000	$41,667	$0
1	$458,333	$41,667	$0
2	$416,667	$41,667	$0
3	$375,000	$41,667	$0
4	$333,333	$41,667	$0
5	$291,667	$41,667	$0
6	$250,000	$41,667	$0
7	$208,333	$41,667	$0
8	$166,667	$41,667	$0
9	$125,000	$41,667	$0
10	$83,333	$41,667	$0
11	$41,667	$41,667	$0
12	$0	$0	$0

Our monthly burn rate therefore is $41,667, which is ($500,000 per team year) / (12 months). This startup has 12 months to get to sustaining revenue, get more funding, or shut down.

The value proposition is obvious: find a scalable business model before the cash is gone. Steve Blank does a great job of addressing this topic in *The Startup Owner's Manual: The Step-By-Step Guide for Building a Great Company*.

In a larger organization, knowing the burn rate (also known as run rate) of an Agile team is your key to understanding how to fund and account for expenditure on a project. To do this, you or your accounting department determines the cost of a persistent team for a defined interval—per week, or per iteration (if your iteration length is consistent and stable). You then compare the burn rate of your teams against the budget for the initiative, product launch, or project completion.

Knowing burn rates can also yield more valuable insights as well. What if you do not have a budget? One of the best managers I've ever worked with once said, "You can't predict when or how you will be judged, just know that you will be." When you are part of a team, your team is burning through money. Someone is watching the money. If you're not watching, you remove yourself from certain types of important conversations for lack of good stewardship. Ignoring financial aspects of your work can cause outcomes as bad as over-focusing on costs can.

Costs vs. Benefits

If you know your burn rate, you can establish—and communicate—a working budget. You can also ask insightful questions about value. For example, if the next 20 things will cost $150,000 to $200,000, based on cycle time or velocity, you can begin a cost/benefits conversation: "Do you think these twenty things will deliver enough value to justify the cost?"

Without fancy, complicated economic models, we have started to quantify value compared to cost. In my experience, these conversations yield far better results when they precede scope and schedule trade-offs. Costs/benefits discussions help us better understand the business constraints (schedule, cost, scope) before determining the suitability of a date.

Business Agility and Lean Thinking

Business agility necessitates applying lean thinking to our enterprise so we can take advantage of Agile development. We create visibility into value streams that allows us to distinguish between work that adds value and work that doesn't. Work that doesn't add value is waste that should be eliminated.

Accounting practices that align with organizational value streams give the people steering the organization the visibility, and levers, they need to keep the organization focused on what matters to the bottom line. This kind of lean accounting is used in lean manufacturing. Cost/benefits analysis within a value stream becomes simpler to attain and evaluate.

IT organizations often categorize their portfolio of investments into models like "Run, Grow, Transform." Companies that have established revenue streams focus first on "keeping the lights on." Increasing cost efficiency certainly has value to the organization. If we can save a million dollars by removing waste in a current value stream, we can use it to invest in other, highly leveraged growth or transformational efforts. If there are assets that support creating new sources of revenue, these may get funded. If not, expect a focus on efficiency improvements to reduce costs. Funded efforts may or may not align to true value streams. It's important to know this because often like pieces of work get grouped together from multiple value streams, which leads to redundancies, inefficiencies, and waste.

Benefits Realization

In this fast-paced world, the cost of delay can be deadly. Benefits realization is a discipline that compares expected value to actual results. Again, if we are clear about what value streams we fund, we can determine how to measure the value.

In traditional organizations, tracking mechanisms are established to evaluate the results, which can take a year or more. In Lean Startup, it is framed in the build-measure-learn cycle. In either case, by reducing batch sizes we can reduce uncertainty and maximize value streams.

Most value-based initiatives, even long-term product efforts, can be funded in increments with intermediate checkpoints. These intermediate check-points should have targets that were agreed upon up-front. They can be based either on hard targets like revenue and market share or softer targets like knowledge creation and market validation.

People need to be confident that they will continue to be funded, assuming they show tangible benefits. By using smaller batches, when cost/benefits indicate we should stop an initiative, the sunk costs are usually low enough that the organization can celebrate the opportunity cost savings and move on.

Asserting Value in Early Phases

To determine the benefits we want to create by investing, we need to have methods to assert a future value. For example, large organizations often have hundreds or thousands of potential opportunities. All of these compete for limited funds. Unlike cost, which is empirical, value is subjective.

So how do you make complex trade-off decisions based on value? There are several methods to choose from, each with its own strengths and weaknesses. None of them work in all circumstances. The ones you choose for knowledge creation may not be the same as for "lights on" activities.

Except in simple cases like replacement technology, traditional return-on-investment (ROI) calculations are riddled with assumptions and favor cost savings efforts. Net Present Value (NPV) and internal rate of return (IRR) are still used as part of business cases and have arguable strengths because they are measured in financial terms that are familiar.

Other prioritization methods promote the use of relative value point estimates or create a matrix to rank against a balanced scorecard through surveys. For example, a relatively new method from Dean Leffingwell's Scaled Agile Framework (SAFe) is the "Weighted Shortest Job First." It is calculated using the sum of relative sizes of (user value + time value + risk reduction)/effort. Relative sizing provides a prioritization mechanism but it can be a "slippery slope." It is potentially incorrect because the wrong sets of people are voting. Also, the values are not in units, such as money, that can be measured later.

Relative prioritization is useful, even though it doesn't always help with benefits realization. If work is funded without measures, then the burden of cost/benefits is relegated to the people doing the work.

Systems engineer and consultant Tom Gilb says, "Demand clear, quantified objectives before happily dispensing money." This is easier with smaller initiatives. I can easily say, "I am willing to spend $100,000 for the next three months to prove or disprove a hypothesis that further investment on capability X could yield K millions of dollars, provided I can estimate the future investment levels needed." This is much more likely to be considered a success whether the hypothesis is right or wrong than to say, "I need 10 million dollars and 16 months, and this will return 40 million dollars in 5 years."

Because value assertions are usually subjective, attempting absolute precision is a bad idea. Instead, focus on small targets that are reasonable, have short timeframes, and are measurable. Whichever methods you choose, remember what the economist John Maynard Keynes once said: "It is better to be roughly right than precisely wrong."

Conclusion
How we spend money is a tangible and visible manifestation of what we value. If we are to reap all the benefits of Agile we need to change our accounting practices to align with Agile and Lean principles.

By applying a simple cost model, we are able to easily infer budgets based on the burn rates of our teams. Once we know our burn rates we can incorporate Lean practices and align our accounting practices to value streams, simplifying cost/benefits analysis significantly—even in complex organizations.

Value-based prioritization is useful but often lacks the data to measure benefits realized. Take the time to assert measurable benefits. Agile teams are some of the most highly disciplined technologists I have had the privilege to meet. When we do not support these knowledge workers and align business practices to our most costly resources, we often lose sight of the true value being delivered. Then, we end up measuring cost but not value delivered. The rest is a slippery slope ...

Planning Releases and Tracking Progress
By Jim Tremlett

Plans are nothing; planning is everything.
—Dwight Eisenhower

Agile development was born out of a mismatch between traditional, big, up-front, activity-based planning processes and the need to be adaptive while responding to dynamic markets. To be adaptive, Agile employs a just-in-time process focused strictly on the delivery of features to customers.

Agile planning is enabled by having stable, persistent teams, and therefore requires that one consider and communicate the context for team-based planning. An important part of this larger context is the longer-range product planning; i.e., how are we going to realize the product over time.

But planning is only half of the equation. Echoing Eisenhower's statement, the management of a development initiative must react to the reality of the development process.

Target—Plan—Commit
When developing a new or existing product, you are continually evolving a product toward your envisioned target. Because it's impossible to develop all the features at once, the planning involves prioritizing the ordering of features and stories you choose to tackle over time. This, of course, requires a commitment by the development team.

I've learned there is no better motivational approach for team ownership than to involve the team in the planning process from the beginning. A team that takes ownership of the development will move heaven and earth to meet its commitment.

Five Levels of Agile Planning
At Rally, we talk about the Five Levels of Agile Planning as depicted in the following figure.

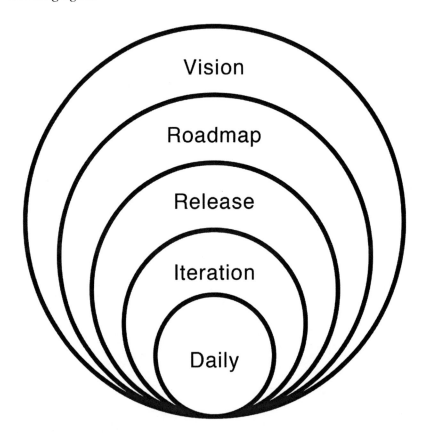

Vision: A concise description of the future product—the product's "True North." This vision should be shared across the product team and be applicable for long stretches of time (6 to 12 months).

Roadmap: This is the roadmap of regularly scheduled feature releases for the product. The era of long delivery cycles is behind us. Customers expect releases on, at least, a quarterly cadence. Often the roadmap maps out a plan of high-level feature releases for the next three to six releases.

Release: This is the plan for delivering the features in the next release. This entails breaking the high-level features into a set of user stories that can be developed by the teams over the course of the iterations that make up the release. For example, if development is employing a 10-week release cadence and 2-week iteration cadence, there will be five iterations within each release.

Iteration: Iteration planning is a Scrum activity that involves breaking the stories planned for that iteration into the tasks needed to realize those stories. Iteration planning includes the commitment by the development team to the plan for the iteration, and the tasking out of stories enables the team to make that commitment.

Daily: In the daily standup and throughout the iteration, the team members coordinate their activities in realizing the stories they have committed to develop.

An important aspect to this process is its just-in-time nature; you don't go into the next level of detailed planning until it's required. Delaying these decisions makes it easier to adapt. You must also consider two important pivot points:

- The **commitment pivot** that, in Scrum, occurs during iteration planning when the team commits to realizing the stories planned for the current iteration
- The **planning pivot** where the set of product features planned for a release is translated into a work plan for the release

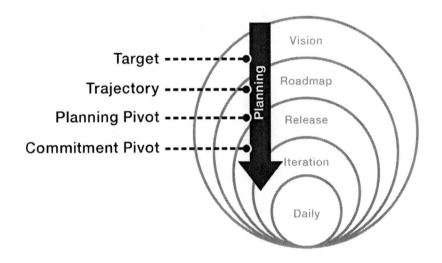

Release Planning: The Pivotal Planning Activity

Release planning is the pivotal planning process in large development initiatives. It's so important because it is the activity that translates the product plan, articulated in the vision and roadmap, into a coordinated work plan for the teams—it's the moment when the translation becomes crystallized.

In addition, the release-planning meeting is a natural setting for team members and stakeholders to interact. This interaction is an example of the Agile preference for face-to-face communications. What's more, the features and high-level stories discussed in release planning offer the right level of detail for engaging stakeholders.

There used to be a car maintenance ad tagline *"Pay me now or pay me later,"* which applies to release planning. The investment the organization makes in release planning is generally recouped in the reduced cost/effort at the iteration planning level.

The Objectives: Features, Stories, and Dependencies

The first objective of release planning is to translate the target features into a set of stories that can be developed across iterations throughout the release. While it's important to keep these stories independent, it's not always possible. Occasionally, the dependencies between user stories impact the timing of the actual story development, which is important to plan for in advance.

As in iteration planning, there is more to release planning than just the planning meeting. The input to the meeting, the backlog, must have been properly groomed in collaboration with the teams—this is a crucial and often forgotten part of the process.

I coach teams to schedule regularly occurring grooming sessions throughout an iteration to ensure the backlog is groomed for the next iteration. I give the same advice to the Product Owner council, which should have a good sense of how the release plan will unfold before the release-planning meeting.

The Final Objective: The Potentially Shippable Increment

The final part of the planning process is to have a coherent set of features that the organization is comfortable releasing to the customer.

This release-level potentially shippable increment (PSI) objective differs from the iteration-level PSI objective. At the iteration level, there shouldn't be any additional work needed on a story (e.g., documentation, testing) before it can be delivered to the customer. However, what is produced in an iteration may not be sufficient for release to the customer. In contrast, by the end, the collection of stories developed in the release should be sufficient for your customer.

Tracking Progress and Reacting to Reality

> *Working Software is the Primary Measure of Progress.*
> —Agile Manifesto

As stated in the introduction, planning is not enough for effective management of product development. There is also the need to adjust plans to reflect internal and external feedback. What does it mean to adapt to the internal reality of the product development?

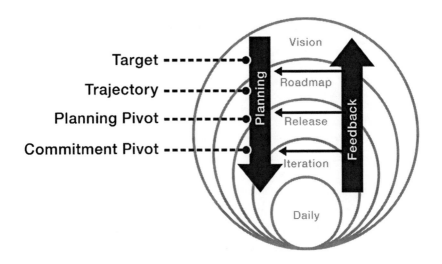

If the teams are not realizing the features/stories planned at each level, the plans must be adjusted. This is an area where Agile development management differs from plan-driven management. In a plan-driven mindset, there has generally been a large investment, so the teams work to push the plan.

In an Agile mindset, you trust that the teams are moving heaven and earth to meet their commitment. When they miss those commitments, the problem is not the effort, it's the plan. Remember, the plan is our best guess at how thing will unfold; if things don't unfold properly, we need to update our guess to reflect reality.

Planning within the five levels of Agile Planning is only half the story. For effective development management, the organization needs to incorporate feedback from the product development. This reaction to internal feedback is an important part of the adaptive nature of Agile development.

Scaling Agile: Fractals of Innovation
By Ronica Roth

"Sure, Agile works for small organizations, but we've got to organize hundreds (or thousands) of people on four continents and Agile just won't work for us." Sound familiar? It does to Rally coaches. It's something we hear all the time, and yet very large companies—all of whom acknowledge that something is wrong with the "traditional" way of doing things—continue to come to us for help.

The challenge we face is not how to create success with their development teams, but how to scale Agile across all teams. This is particularly difficult because we must factor in the many different things done in the organization, including product roadmapping, funding, system architecture, and release planning.

Sound daunting? The good news is you needn't reinvent it all for your organization. An excellent starting point has been developed in the Scaled Agile Framework, recently released by Dean Leffingwell. SAFe, as it's called, has been tested in many large enterprises, including some of Rally's biggest customers.

As with existing Agile frameworks like Scrum and XP, you'll want to start with the core prescriptive elements and adjust for your environment as you learn and change.

Scaling by Fractals

Scaling Agile means that we apply its principles to large, even very large, groups of people. When we do this, we allow those people to be more connected to their work and its impact, despite being part of a huge system.

This process is effective because we scale Agile by fractals, meaning we create similarly shaped structures at different levels of scale throughout the organization. And rather than build bigger teams, we add more small, cross-functional teams and stitch them together into a larger whole. This way, the team remains the core unit and owns its working agreements, information radiators, and policies.

As you might expect, it's not quite enough to simply add teams. Those teams will need leadership to guide them, a structure to align them, and information to enable Agile's continuous improvement.

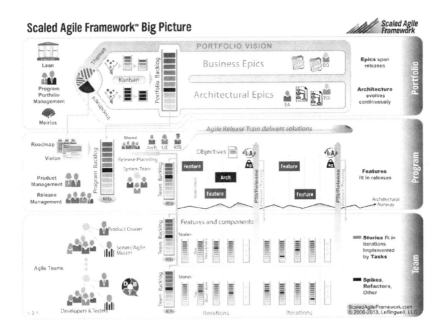

For an interactive version of this graphic visit: scaledagileframework.com

Cadence and Synchronization

In order to effectively coordinate work with many teams, you must look three to six iterations down the line. And to do this effectively, your teams need to have worked together for a while. These mid-range plans, sometimes called *release plans*, need not be perfect of course, but by creating a certain level of predictability you remove the risk from coordination and delivery.

Once we have a team with a cadence of iteration and release planning, we add several Agile teams, each with 5 to 10 people. The number of teams depends on who is needed in order to build and deliver a system of value. This helps determine how many teams make up the *program*.

While it's usually obvious which individuals make up a program, some organizations struggle with creating smaller, cross-functional teams. If you find yourself in this situation, provide your employees with the boundary conditions and let them divvy up the teams together.

Those teams must now coordinate their work in two key ways: by ensuring their delivered work adds up to valuable features, and by managing dependencies between them. Teams achieve this by synchronizing their cadences, and planning and retrospecting together.

With every team running tested software by the end of each iteration, we have a clean synchronization point. This system isn't perfect, but it's far easier than systems used in traditional phased development.

As for ensuring all the work leads to value, the key is to host a joint release-planning event that includes all the members of each team. This event is designed as a way to check on each team's plans and make important adjustments.

SAFe describes the Scrum release timebox as a potentially shippable increment, or PSI. Even if your group will never release software so frequently, this mid-range planning horizon is critical to quality, coordination, and success.

Support Structures

Synchronized teams still need supporting roles and structures beyond themselves in order to coordinate effectively and deliver value. SAFe defines several of these, which are outlined below. But you'll need to define the right structures and roles for your own organization.

Building the right thing: How can all those team-level Product Owners (POs) make sure their backlogs of stories add up to value? Product Managers (PMs), who own the backlog of Features at the Program level, meet regularly with Product Owners to ensure shared vision and understanding. This way, POs can make adjustments in their own backlogs at a later date, confident they continue to support the shared vision.

Building the thing right: The System Team (ST) owns care and feeding of the whole system, while the Release Management Team (RMT) ensures the success of each release. Architecture is a first-class citizen in SAFe, and a program roadmap of features also includes architecture deliverables.

Building the whole thing: Among other structures and roles, SAFe adds the so-called Release Train Engineer (RTE)—an "uberScrumMaster" who helps teams coordinate deliveries, communicate, escalate problems, manage risk, and continuously improve at the program level. The RTE helps keep the train on the tracks. In your organization, these people might be called project managers, program managers, or development managers.

The Role of Leadership
Strong leadership—not management—is essential to helping Agile work at this scale.

To lead, on one level, is to provide a clear vision around what the program is trying to achieve. This vision gets created, and can be trusted, in part by injecting Agile discipline and visibility at the portfolio and program levels. That means, for example, funding fewer initiatives and limiting work in process rather than filling development queues with wishful thinking.

We apply similar rigor to steering decisions. Agile portfolio management emphasizes steering over planning. Having funded an initiative, and seeing the early results of execution, the portfolio council decides—on a cadence—whether to continue, to adjust, or to kill each initiative. Those decisions tell the teams that their learnings are appreciated and heard.

The whole system, from top (portfolio) to bottom (team) and from left (business) to right (DevOps and Support), is ultimately about learning and creating feedback loops.

To facilitate innovation and performance, leaders from the very top of the organization must build a culture of learning.

At the team and program levels, organizational leaders are responsible for coaching their people on the tools of continuous improvement and encouraging them to relentlessly improve. For it's only when employees see the vision for their work and have all the necessary information that they'll feel truly empowered to act.

Steering the Agile Enterprise
with Kanban Thinking
By Karl Scotland

Kanban Thinking is the framework I use when approaching the design of a Kanban System within a given context. The central concept is that the design approach is based on principles of Systems Thinking.

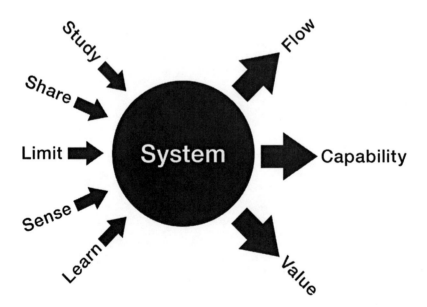

Kanban Thinking looks to eliminate delays rather than eliminate waste. What's more, the goal is to maximize value rather than minimize cost, and to develop people as problem solvers rather than develop tools to solve problems. To get a better understanding of the process, the figure on the previous page shows the anticipated impacts the system design should have: flow, value, and capability.

The Portfolio as a System

As a system, a portfolio is more than the sum of its parts—the initiatives, projects, features, teams, and people—but is a product of the interactions of those parts with a particular tendency. Managing a portfolio, and as a result steering the enterprise, is the job of designing and guiding the portfolio such that its tendency is to have a positive impact.

Portfolio Levers

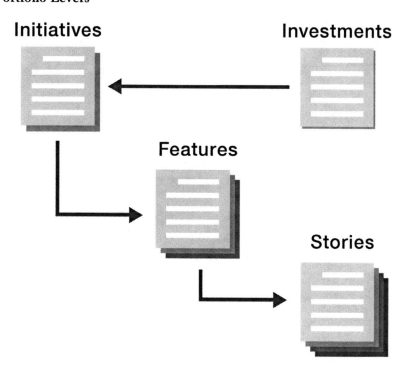

Studying

When studying an existing portfolio, it is useful to begin by identifying all that is known about the work. That work can then be clustered and arranged into themes based on similarity or relatedness. Common patterns that emerge are often based around investment and work item types, hierarchies, and their governance workflow.

Examples of investment types might be areas such as system architecture, urgent customer requests, current market segments, expanding market segments, or future opportunities. Those investment types might include initiatives, which are progressed through the development of features, which are iterated on by breaking down into stories.

Sharing

Sharing a portfolio involves creating a model of the work that everyone can easily access and understand. Kanban boards—visual depictions of the Kanban system—are simple, powerful tools for illustrating how the system works.

The most common approach is to create columns for the various stages of workflow. For example, initiatives might begin as options, then have some discovery work done, then be assessed for suitability, then built and released before the results are reviewed for learning.

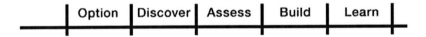

An important question to ask when designing the mechanism that will be used to share the portfolio is what you want to understand in order to learn. The TIP (Token, Inscription, Placement) heuristic is a useful tool to help you think about how to amplify the important signals and dampen any noise.

Limiting

Limiting a portfolio is the means by which it can be effectively steered. By limiting the number of initiatives or features being worked on, they can be completed sooner and with greater predictability, which allows organizations to get earlier feedback and better respond to new information and changing market conditions.

Work can be limited at a number of levels. Investment allocation can help keep the portfolio focused on the right mix of work. The number of initiatives and features can be limited to focus on finishing work before new work is started. Flowing work through stable teams can be used to balance demand against the capacity and capability of those teams.

In addition to using a portfolio Kanban system to limit work in process, explicit policies also can limit work. Creating transparency of the boundaries of the system design means that the system can be stable within those constraints, and that the policies can be evolved to allow the system to evolve. A simple approach to policies is to add a checklist of exit criteria to each stage of the workflow.

	Option	Discover	Assess	Build	Learn
Exit Policy					
Limit	5	3	2	3	4

Sensing

Sensing the performance of the portfolio is what tells us how well it is being steered, so that direction can be adjusted effectively. There are generally two elements to sensing: establishing a cadence and measuring outcomes.

Establishing a cadence creates a sense of rhythm and helps reduce the co-ordination cost of getting people together. Regular meetings that mesh with the cadence can be used to plan and review the portfolio, and to gather new information and feedback. A portfolio council can be created to schedule and prioritize work in a timely manner, and to ensure the focus is on the most important work.

Establishing appropriate measures generates insights that can aid decision making about what can be done to enable better outcomes. For a portfolio Kanban system, financial measure seems to be appropriate. An economic model that uses high-level estimates of the costs and benefits of initiatives or features, along with an understanding of the run-rate of teams, allows effective trade-off to be made between portfolio items. A timeline of planned and actual progress, for example, provides the basis for a rolling forecast as an alternative to annual plans.

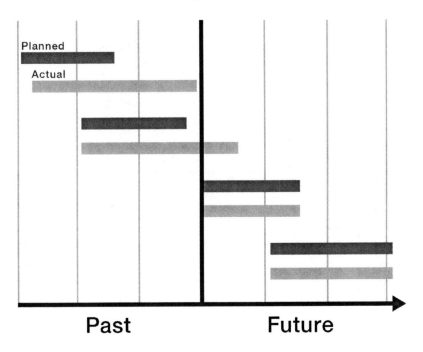

Past   Future

Learning
Whatever choices you make, the design of your portfolio Kanban system, and the work within it, will be wrong. Learning—the detection and correction of those errors—is key to evolving the portfolio so that it has a greater, more positive impact.

Steering a portfolio is about updating the portfolio to match the reality of the current situation, rather than managing the portfolio toward a future situation. By sensing current performance with a regular cadence, work can be advanced, delayed, or even killed to keep focus on the most important work.

Evolving a portfolio Kanban system is about running deliberate experiments, with prediction and validation of how changes to the system design will affect its impact. Again, by sensing current performance with a regular cadence, visualizations, WIP limits, and other explicit policies, a portfolio can be adjusted as knowledge is gained about what a better design should be.

Portfolio Impact

Flow

Achieving flow across a portfolio Kanban system means that the initiatives, programs, projects, or features in the system progress with as few delays as possible. As a result, the enterprise will be able to respond appropriately and quickly to the competitive landscape. Further, when flow is smooth across a portfolio, the work delivered by the system becomes more reliable and lead times become easier to predict.

Value

Delivering value from a portfolio Kanban system means the initiatives, programs, projects, or features in the system are the most important things that could be worked on at that time. As a result, stakeholder satisfaction will increase as customers get their needs met. Maintaining stakeholder satisfaction sustainably means that quality will also increase.

Capability

Building capability with a portfolio Kanban system means that the right initiatives, programs, projects, or features can be effectively delivered over the long term, not just the short term. As a result, employee satisfaction will increase, leading to greater retention of people and their knowledge. This long-term building of people, teams, and their skills will also lead to an increase in overall productivity.

Conclusion

Steering the Agile Enterprise means looking at the whole portfolio, and continuously adjusting priorities, focus, and investments. Kanban Thinking provides a lens through which to view the portfolio in order to help guide both decision making and evaluating the result of those decisions. Studying, sharing, limiting, sensing, and learning are activities that help us have an impact on the portfolio. Flow, value, and capability are the factors that let us know if we're having a positive impact.

By treating the portfolio as a system, we allow trade-offs to be made at the right level and avoid decisions being made without direct observation or experience. This not only maximizes the value we create, it also builds a system that can learn, grow, and adapt to changing conditions.

Retrospectives:
The Heartbeat of Continuous Improvement
By Ken Clyne

Agile is an empirical approach. We regularly take stock of how we're doing, then adapt and change course as we learn. This is very different from making a plan and sticking to it in hopes that what transpires will be valuable.

This approach is more than a mere preference; it is a business necessity. We simply can't know everything up front. Our markets are too chaotic and our products too complex. Change, therefore, is good.

However, the wrong change, change for change's sake, or too much change all at once can be both wasteful and distracting. Lean Manufacturing teaches us that we attain higher levels of productivity, quality, and value when the degree of change is relatively small and continuous. This is called Kaizen.

This spirit of continuous improvement is at the heart of one of the 12 principles of the Agile Manifesto: *At regular intervals, the team reflects on how to become more effective, then tunes and adjusts its behavior accordingly.*

This is what's called the Retrospective, and it can take multiple forms.

In its simplest form, we spend a few moments at the conclusion of key Agile ceremonies, such as iteration planning or iteration reviews, to reflect on what just occurred and what opportunities we might have for improving our time together.

Heartbeat Retrospectives occur on a regular cadence, usually at the conclusion of iterations. They typically take between one to two hours and allow us to dive deeper into what we can change to improve for the next time.

Timeline Retrospectives reflect over a longer period of time, such as a quarter or in response to some significant event—good or bad.

Regardless of the form it takes, every retrospective needs to be grounded in **safety and trust**. In his book *Project Retrospectives*, Norm Kerth offers up his prime directive as a working agreement to set the stage for every retrospective ritual:

"Regardless of what we discover, we understand and truly believe that everyone did the best job they could, given what they knew at the time, their skills and abilities, the resources available, and the situation at hand."

In their book *Switch: How to Change Things When Change Is Hard*, Chip and Dan Heath point out that of the 24 most common "emotion" words in the English language, only 6 of those words are positive. Yes, we have a predilection for the negative and it can be difficult to **pursue bright spots** and ask: "What's working and how can we do more of it?"

We need to establish a **rhythm of continuous improvement** and make a promise to ourselves and to others that we will follow through and implement any changes agreed upon. We must also have the organizational discipline to proceed through successive small improvements and not try to change too much too soon. If we aim too high we run the risk that failure becomes our habit.

Most Agile organizations have already institutionalized the Retrospective. However, we must not be complacent. While it is very difficult to create an environment of continuous improvement, it is remarkably simple to destroy one.

Agile Contracts

By Michael Ball-Marian

One of the most powerful benefits of Agile is its adaptability. Still, some companies believe that Agile may not be the best fit for their organization. This objection is often heard in organizations where development is governed by a legal contract—either with an internal partner in the same organization or with an outside vendor.

There are two common problems faced by contract-based organizations, and both are really opportunities in disguise.

One concern is that Agile doesn't work well with fixed-bid proposals—a highly requested and utilized contract. But that simply isn't the case. As long as the contract allows for flexibility of scope, Agile can actually deliver far superior business results.

Another misconception is that Agile comes from internal product development or IT organizations, and thus many practices won't work well in a contract organization. The key here is to focus on executing the values and culture of Agile while also inspecting and adapting the practices to your organization's needs.

One example of this, common in an agency setting, is visual design. Traditionally, this is done largely up front, with many costly rounds of mockups and customer input before a line of code is written. Adapting this to Agile means establishing some minimal design patterns up front (to understand the customer's vision), with detailed design evolving (iteratively) as the project progresses.

Presented well, Agile can be seen by customers as an opportunity to avoid the frustrations encountered with a traditional contract approach. Customers love that Agile welcomes their involvement, encourages scope changes, handles them efficiently, and helps avoid waste. What's more, many customers are delighted to learn they will receive actual working software early and regularly throughout the project.

The trick is to not get caught up in explaining the minutiae of Agile process—customers don't care about "process." Instead, it's more effective to accentuate the results they will see, the control they will have, and the visibility they will achieve.

The heart of Agile is its adaptive nature. It has successfully been adapted to many environments, including contract-based projects or engagements.

Stickies, Sharpies, and Information Radiators
By Jeff Ellis

Stickies (or Post-it notes) may seem like a simple tool for capturing quick ideas, but in Agile organizations, they can have a mighty effect when collecting input in retrospectives, planning meetings, and brainstorming new ideas.

During designated meetings, participants write their thoughts on stickies, present them to the team, and attach them to a whiteboard. Once all of the input has been collected, the team prioritizes and organizes the stickies by moving them around on the board using various organizational techniques. Finally, participants volunteer to "take the action" by retrieving a sticky to be worked on outside of the meeting.

Below is a list of best practices that can help your team get the most out of this valuable tool:

- Stock the room with plenty of stickies of various sizes and colors.
- Write one story/note/idea on each sticky. This allows them to be prioritized or delegated separately.
- Use Sharpies (not ballpoint pens) on the stickies so that they can be read from a distance.
- Keep the Sharpies far away from the whiteboards! Make sure they're kept separate from whiteboard markers.

- Buy porcelain or glass whiteboards. The plastic kind will quickly stain to the point of being unusable.

- Take a photo of the whiteboard after the meeting with a mobile phone and email the image to the participants as the "meeting minutes."

- If you must write "do not erase" on a whiteboard, add the date and your name.

- If the meeting includes remote participants, consider using an online tool for collecting and organizing information on the stickies so that everyone can participate.

The Daily Standup

By André Dhondt

One of the biggest challenges we face when doing something complex, like building a piece of software, is coordinating action in an effective way. While enterprise communication tools and formal processes and protocols can be helpful, we often overlook the simplest and most effective tool at our disposal: conversation. The Daily Standup can help teams of any level deliver more value in the fastest and least stressful way possible. Here's how it works:

At least once a day, teams hold a Daily Standup to adjust priorities based on new learnings, risks, and obstacles. The goal, of course, is to stay focused on both the individual and team goals. This is a time to assess the team's priorities.

Before the Standup, each team member considers what colleagues may be interested in, and finds a way to express this information concisely. Think of each Standup announcement as a quick and easy way to incite action or feedback. This may prompt the team members to help one another, react to a change, or ask for help from somebody in a different group. Since a Daily Standup is limited to 15 minutes, we can't go into detail or debate.

On occasion, simple decisions, rapid updates to iteration plans, or requests for simple feedback may be included. If consensus is not reached within 60 seconds, the team will schedule the discussion for another time. This rescheduling is called "taking it offline," or putting it in the "parking lot."

Distilled messages increase the team members' ability to stay engaged and identify ways they can participate, increasing team capacity.

Avoid treating the Daily Standup as a status meeting or as a report to managers. Conversely, don't let the manager derail the team's focus with his or her own agenda. The manager's main job during a Standup is to take notes and identify what's working and what isn't.

Remember, this meeting is for the team.

The Sprint Review and Demo

By Eric Willeke

Congratulations! You're done! You've delivered! Now it's time to show off what you've done, and you don't even have to wait for the end of a yearlong release. You've reached the end of a two-week iteration, and it's time for the ceremony named "Sprint Review." It's important to see this as a chance to show off and celebrate in front of your entire group of extended stakeholders, and we should also acknowledge the other important roles Sprint Review plays in helping effective teams drive forward.

In essence, Sprint Review has two parts, the last being a conversation between the entire Scrum team and the various stakeholders. I like to split out the first part as "the review" and call the rest "the demo" because I think people tend to overlook the first item on the agenda, where we stand up and say, "We committed to these eight items, and we finished the following seven." The rest of the meeting consists of the team sharing work the product owner has accepted during the Sprint and discussing potential ideas for future work based on stakeholder reactions.

I feel the first step is critical because of the closure it provides around the commitment that was made at the beginning of a Sprint. This brings additional weight to the commitment and reminds the room that: "This was the commitment we made. No more, and no less. Here's how we fared." Beyond this moment, the rest of the meeting helps demonstrate to the team members that their company values their contributions, and that both the team and product owner are able to see and hear what's on the stakeholders' minds, leading to less confusion around changes that show up in the backlog after the meeting. Additionally, the emotional reactions of stakeholders during the demo provide great feedback for the retrospective: "Did you see Kelly's face when we showed the sorting transitions? She was pumped! I'm glad we focused on making those smooth."

Oh, and don't forget to celebrate. You've earned it!

5

Transform Your Organization

Transform Your Organization
By Bob Gower

We are what we repeatedly do. Excellence, then, is not an act, but a habit.
—Will Durant (on Aristotle)

In 1987, when Paul O'Neill took over as CEO of Alcoa—a once great giant of American industry—he vowed to put all his energy behind improving one metric and one metric only: worker safety.

When his tactics were questioned by a group of concerned investors, he explained, "If we bring our injury rates down, it won't be because of cheerleading or the nonsense you sometimes hear from other CEOs. It will be because the individuals at this company have agreed to become part of something important: They've devoted themselves to creating a habit of excellence."

O'Neill chose safety as his metric—instead of profits, efficiency, inventory, or cost of goods sold—because he recognized that safety is core to culture and that culture in turn is core to success. Transform the culture, he believed, and you'd transform the bottom line.

And he was right. In his 12 years as CEO, there was not only a dramatic reduction in worker injuries and deaths, there was an incredible improvement in business performance. Alcoa's net income multiplied by a factor of five, and market capitalization increased by a staggering $27 billion. If you'd invested a million dollars in Alcoa on the day O'Neill took over, you would have earned another million in dividends alone by the time he left.

A Silver Bullet?

If you're reading this book you likely want to change your organization. And, if you're like most leaders I talk to, you regularly evaluate processes and tools that presumably will give you some combination of the following: better products, less waste, and happier workers. This in turn leads to happier customers, a healthier bottom line, and, perhaps, personal glory.

But you don't really want a new process—and trust me, your people don't want another "change initiative." What you want is a new culture, a culture of excellence.

The reason Agile values "individuals and interactions over processes and tools" is that building cultures that empower individuals to shine and contribute are durable and productive. They also require far less management overhead to maintain than do heavyweight, draconian processes. We start with the assumption that humans actually want to provide value for each other. Then we work to organically grow organizations that harness this desire.

Agile processes and tools are actually install mechanisms for culture. By requesting that people work together in certain ways, track specific metrics, and check in with each other at specified intervals, we put in place the building blocks for people to interact in positive, productive ways.

Far from a silver bullet, these processes and tools are more like silver mirrors that help us see the organization, customer, and product clearly. It's only when operating from this point of clarity that we're able to make changes to an ever-evolving process. This is what leads to an organization becoming what Peter Senge calls a *learning organization*, one that is capable of improving continuously over time.

How to Change

The first step to change is of course discomfort; change is difficult, messy, and challenging. In fact, most people will avoid any kind of change unless the current situation is uncomfortable on a personal level. But what do you do once you've made the decision to make a change and go through the discomfort and inevitable immediate loss in productivity that working with a new process will bring? How do you bring legitimate change to your organization?

Prevailing wisdom is often that the *fish rots from the head* and starts with the organization's leadership team. While it's tempting to start at the top, spending too much time and energy converting the CEO and leadership team is an expensive and slow process that runs a real risk of failure.

A popular alternative to top-down change is what veteran Lean theorist and consultant Don Reinertsen calls the *Wildfire Model*, where we depend on grassroots efforts within the organization to catch fire and combine into sweeping organizational change. While cheaper and less risky than doing things top down, this method doesn't have a mechanism to address organizational impediments or coordinate effort. It harnesses people's enthusiasm, but without some central support these fires frequently reach organizational limits and burn themselves out, leaving people even more demoralized and resistant to change than they were before—if they remain with the organization at all.

At Rally, we've come to value an approach that creates a collaborative working group—often called the Agile Rollout Team or Agile Working Group—that manages and coordinates the backlog of transformation activities across the organization. This group's members come primarily from the middle of the organization—functional managers, project managers, and product managers. It creates a vision of where the organization would like to go, then sets specific goals, and launches pilot programs with the intention of learning and dynamically steering the change effort. How fast or slowly the change can happen depends on what's learned along the way about what's easy and what's difficult in this particular organization.

Shifts in Leadership Behavior
While we want to proceed organically and collaboratively, one of the most powerful things an organization can do is encourage a shift in leadership behavior.

As we ask other people to become more engaged in their work, more empathetic with customers, and more creative in their solutions, we need to listen more and do less. And to do this, we must slay our own demons of FUD (Fear, Uncertainty, and Doubt) and develop a greater trust.

Often the support of a coach or a colleague from outside the organization is key to this personal transformation. As renowned physicist Richard Feynman used to say, "The first principle is that you must not fool yourself, and you are the easiest person to fool." Trusted advisors are essential to helping us understand when we're fooling ourselves.

Shifts in the Organization
If we're to create sustained change in our organizations, the focus can't be only on our behavior or attitudes as leaders. We must also look at the structures of the organization that impede—or aid—the adoption of new, better behaviors. The two most effective areas to examine are the ways we measure projects and organize teams.

Rewards drive behavior. Many organizations use explicit and implicit metrics that measure and reward the amount of code written, the amount of time people spend in their chairs or the amount of stress—which often looks like hard work to detached managers—people encounter. These measures often unintentionally drive the wrong behaviors—people coming in early and leaving late to impress the boss but goofing off while at their desks.

A shift to an organizational structure made up of interlocking and interdependent teams allows us to harness the power of shared commitment. Teams that commit together to deliver to another team—or an external customer—are more likely to perform well. This is because you can't get lost on a small team; your teammates see your work, or lack thereof, and hold each other accountable. These loose social ties and obligations that bind small groups together have been shown repeatedly in research to be much stronger motivators than any bureaucratic reward or punishment.

Teams simultaneously support us and hold us accountable. As I write this, I'm aware that I need to pass this piece off to an editor today. I'm free to do the work in a cafe (I'm in one in Brooklyn now), at my home, or at an office I've rented in Manhattan. However, I'm not free to simply finalize the work on my own with no accountability or oversight, nor would I want to. Knowing I have a team to comment on my work and hold me accountable to a certain level of timeliness and quality helps me do better work. I also know that I have some really smart people to lean on when I'm not sure how to approach a problem or when I face a time crunch.

Take It Home

I encourage you to develop ideas about experiments you can run and changes you can make, sooner rather than later. How can you apply these ideas tomorrow or next week instead of next quarter or next year? How can you begin to adopt the stance of a curious student and willing participant in transforming your organization?

If you start there, you can develop the culture of continual growth and learning that separates organizations of excellence from those of mere mediocrity.

Flow-Pull-Innovate—Your Agile Journey

By Ryan Martens

If you want to build a ship, don't drum up the men to gather the wood, divide the work, and give orders. Instead, teach them to yearn for the sea.

—Antoine de Saint-Exupery

As you begin to "get" Agile, you start to understand the notion of steering with small, fast, iterative, and incremental efforts. You see the waste in big batches, the costs in context switching, and the value of a cross-functional team that can converge quickly on complex problems. You start to curse the manufacturing metaphor and hang instead on metaphors of restaurants and theater.

I met one senior engineering manager who said that he was like the kid from the film *The Sixth Sense*. Instead of being able to see dead people, he could walk around and see waste everywhere. An Agilist like this understands that it's a journey—not a destination that you reach with a single silver bullet.

I like to talk about this journey using Jim Collins's popular book *Good to Great*. I see the adoption of Agile as a journey toward Great. As Collins points out, to get to Great you must both increase your agility and your discipline. In the software development world, you must shorten cycle time and increase automation to move up the ladder to Great.

Good to Great

Hierarchical

Culture of
Discipline

Great
Business

High

Innovate

Pull

Low | Waterfall | Flow | High | Agility and Innovation

Standing Still | Chaos

Low

Bureaucratic

Heroism

If you buy my assertion that this is a journey, then you can also agree that a successful journey has the potential to create capacity in the people and organization while also increasing the speed of learning.

The results that I've seen from our customers over the last eight years indicate that impact happens quickly and has a powerful cumulative effect. And the "2011 Chaos Manifesto," a report by IT consultancy Standish Group, showed that software applications developed through the Agile process have three times the success rate of the traditional waterfall method. In addition, these applications have a much lower percentage of time and cost overruns. Lately, some of Agile's largest customers have been telling us they've experienced a threefold to fourfold increase in productivity, quality, and employee engagement.

In an attempt to describe the strategy behind your Agile journey, Jean Tabaka, Rally's Agile Fellow, and I have developed a simple map to shape your trip. We call it Flow-Pull-Innovate. These incremental steps provide the focus and attention of the journey. To break those increments into smaller iterations, we cross-reference those steps with organizational scale to form a nine-square grid that allows you to map your steps from bottom left to top right.

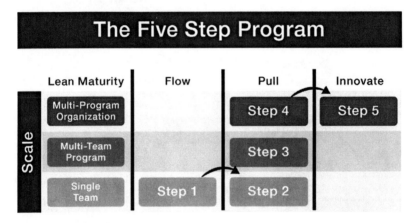

Notice this map does not talk about time or scope. Since 2004, most Agile adoptions have started with pilots and moved incrementally through these steps.

The successful adoption path for Agile is evolutionary, not revolutionary. No team or teams or organization can adopt it all in a single jump. Teams need to apply the principles and well-defined sets of practices using an incremental and iterative approach before applying them throughout the organization. As an organization gets better at the basic set of Agile disciplines at the team level, it can then move up the Agile evolutionary ladder based on success, realization of benefits, and confidence.

Consider the simple discipline of how Agile scales teams. Agile scales its disciplines and practices through the replication of teams, rather than through increasing the size of existing teams. This requires that organizations invest first in multiple cross-functional teams, extend the Agile disciplines to manage many synchronized teams, and finally grow these disciplines to manage beyond the development teams. This discipline relies on organizational growth without growing the size of its teams. No productive team will consist of more than seven to nine people. Once a team reaches that size, Agile discipline requires that a new team split off from the current one.

In 2009, we started seeing bold efforts that went "all in" and jumped from early pilots to Step 4 in one giant leap. Now with the addition of Agile portfolio management methods and enterprise solutions like Rally, these major leaps have become more common. However, executing this approach requires lots of preparation, coaching, tools, and coordination/training at the team, program management, and executive levels.

The real question is: How far do you want to get by when?

No matter if you pause on each step or make major leaps, I strongly suggest that you work through all of the following steps with at least one program or product:

Step 1—Single-Team Flow: We recommend all Agile adoptions start by enabling *flow* in a single, cross-functional team. *Flow* means that a team is able to rapidly and smoothly carry small batches of work from idea to production. This step illuminates the value Agile brings, and helps identify the missing technical infrastructure needed to promote Agility. More broadly, it also helps the organization understand the changes to culture and workflow that need to occur throughout the organization. The enthusiasm and success of this first small group typically encourage the creation of more pilot teams and inspire them to increase effectiveness, not just efficiency.

Step 2—Single-Team Pull: In Pull, a team starts to sequence the work in ways that increase learning and decrease risk. Team members are no longer simply trying to build the thing right but are moving to understand what the right thing to build is. They work to interact frequently with real customers and leverage feedback benefits by dampening features that are less valuable and amplifying those that are more valuable. At this point in the Agile adoption, managers start to see some amazing value from better decision making, such as higher quality and smoother flow of work. You now have a working model for how to scale this organizationally to a major project, program, or product level.

Step 3—Program Pull: This step starts with the deployment of new infrastructure and staff training to coordinate efforts that require multiple teams. Program Management teams and Product Management organizations must now be fully engaged in Agile efforts on a day-to-day basis. With middle-management support and the technical infrastructure for distributed team management and rapid deployment in place, you have a recipe for getting better solutions, not just features, into customers' hands as fast as possible. This typically translates into large cost savings, but also revenue increases. I have seen triple or quadruple increases in efficiency and effectiveness improvements that dwarf productivity improvements. You also now have a pattern and infrastructure for replicating this in multiple programs.

Step 4—Enterprise Pull: Enterprise Pull scales Agile by replicating in multiple programs, and it also increases the scope of the Agile journey. Scope typically increases in the portfolio management process, business strategy, operations, and marketing. Overall, the typical project or product stage-gate model starts to wane. Given the added visibility, shortened cycle times, and flexibility found in pull-based Agile development organizations, the portfolio management process becomes more about steering the flow of work than planning and resource allocation. This transition provides the business with much more frequent opportunities to make small portfolio adjustments based on real market feedback. This starts to translate into much better insights and decisions and thus better company performance. At this point, you can see your Agile journey beginning to change your overall corporate culture, not just your development organization.

Step 5—Innovate: The state of Innovate focuses on reinvesting some of the newfound capacity of the system to increase the flow of innovation to the market. The capacity comes from providing slack in the system to allow for more experimentation. The decrease in overall work-in-process found by adopting Agile portfolio approaches increases the slack and flexibility in development. Using it for more experimentation and innovation is only tolerable when a program or product is winning in the eyes of the customers. Otherwise, the traditional portfolio approach will tend to expand scope to fill all available development cycles. This is why we don't typically see a push toward a culture of innovation until Step 5. However, it is very common to send some scout teams into Innovate during Step 4, so they can learn the ways of continuous innovation and create the organizational yearning.

I believe this map helps Agile Champions, like you, communicate the Agile journey in a more comprehensive way and shed light on the four critical elements that leaders must use to serve their organization on their Agile journey:

1. A vision for being a great organization
2. A roadmap of incremental steps across this Flow-Pull-Innovate map
3. A social contract for the employees with regard to what is in it for them
4. A visible commitment to the journey

If you follow this approach, I know you will gain great business results, while also developing a newfound enjoyment for your work. But most important, you will learn how to build great solutions that improve our society, life, and planet.

A Path to Agility
By Ronica Roth

At Rally, we've been working for more than 10 years to help organizations be more Agile. We're continually evolving our understanding of how to do this and we revise our models frequently based on what we learn out there in the field—inside companies large and small who want better products, happier people, and faster, more predictable release schedules.

Over the years we have found a path to enterprise Agility that reduces risk, builds in learning loops, and allows everyone to play a part in defining the new organization.

We find that Agile transformations are best approached in an Agile manner. That is, they must be flexible—we serve organizations of all shapes, sizes, and cultures—and prescriptive enough that we don't get lost along the way. So we view Agile adoption as a journey of discovery. Over the years, we've mapped a route that allows you to move forward in your Agile adoption without dictating exactly what your Agile implementation will look like.

This pathway includes four phases, with specific organizational changes—and benefits—that occur in each. It's designed to help an organization adopt Agile iteratively and incrementally, starting with a couple small, independent Agile teams and expanding to coordinate the work of many.

By following this path and learning to adjust as you go, you will build an organization of passionate and engaged problem solvers and innovators.

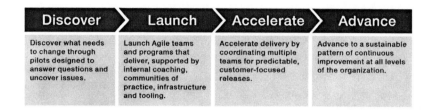

Discover — Discover what needs to change through pilots designed to answer questions and uncover issues.

Launch — Launch Agile teams and programs that deliver, supported by internal coaching, communities of practice, infrastructure and tooling.

Accelerate — Accelerate delivery by coordinating multiple teams for predictable, customer-focused releases.

Advance — Advance to a sustainable pattern of continuous improvement at all levels of the organization.

Why It Works

Agile adoption—even for companies whose culture already predisposes them to Agile—is fraught with all the risk of organizational change. Our path to Agility helps you manage that risk through learning, incremental outcomes, and collaboration. What's more, it helps reduce the structural risk that comes with any Agile adoption and helps each organization discover how to change the way it builds and delivers a product while continuing to meet commitments.

I worked with a large Internet retailer during the first 18 months of its Agile rollout. One huge structural question was how to handle the final test and release of incrementally developed code. By starting the rollout with just a few Agile teams spread across several code areas, we carefully built learning around the improved quality of those teams' work and developed a new, Agile release process everyone could trust.

There is, of course, also a people risk when executing an Agile adoption. Some people embrace change quickly and eagerly while others warm slowly to change or resist it altogether. It's important to anticipate this risk and create a solution before it becomes a challenge.

Years ago, I worked with a midsize finance firm that was rolling out Scrum. Every couple months I visited suburban Detroit to launch two more teams. To help add clarity to the process, the first morning of each visit I would spend an hour giving a quick Agile overview, which was open to anyone in the company. Attendees included folks from human resources, customer service, finance, and other departments. The short overview explained why the company was changing its development process, what it would look like for everyone, and offered a basic vocabulary translation.

In just one hour, I watched the attendees evolve emotionally from worried and confused to calm and relaxed. They had been included in a promising initiative to improve the company, and now they welcomed the new process.

How to Do It

Like many worthwhile journeys, the path to Agility starts with identifying a critical and urgent goal. Once the goal has been articulated, we need a cross-functional group of leaders to own the initiative. This team is responsible for the outcome of the project and thus has the responsibility of planning and adjusting the path.

The team begins the journey with Discovery, which is done through pilots that help everyone get to "flow" and provide key learnings for the future. Armed with these learnings, the team defines success and lays out a roadmap, which ideally answers many of the following questions:

- Which divisions/groups will reorganize and change their methodology?
- What training and coaching support will be provided?
- Which projects and programs will be run using Agile?
- What Agile scaling structures will be added?
- What improvements (with measures) will we expect to see?

Now you're ready to run monthly "iterations" of your Agile adoption, which support the Launch phase. During these iterations, new Agile teams will have the opportunity to get good enough at Agile to deliver on mid-range commitments with high quality. In the process, you'll begin creating a new structure that puts testers, developers, business analysts, and others on the same team.

As you support and Retrospect on Launch iterations, your adoption team will help the organization change to support Agile. You might guide the emergence of new development standards, visibility tools, or communication paths.

Early learnings will support the move into the **Accelerate** phase, where the rate of change and value delivery begin to speed up. We add new processes, structures, and roles in order to coordinate the work of many teams to deliver bigger features and programs.

In this phase, you might need to change a lot of technical infrastructure to support large coordinated releases. You may need to expand Agile education out to business partners in the company, so they can support a continuous, value-driven delivery model. You might retool the PMO to support strategic, Agile initiatives. Once this is complete, you're ready to enter the **Advance** phase.

The Advance phase is really the moment you realize there was no destination, no end-state of "doing Agile 100 percent." Instead, you'll see that "being Agile" means always seeing ways to improve and always responding to those opportunities in an Agile way. People will take ownership of problems, seek collaborators to design responses, and strive to run small experiments or effect increments of change.

In the Advance phase, your "Agile Transformation Team" changes membership and becomes a "Continuous Improvement Team" that helps the company see the opportunities and prioritize them.

In the words of psychologist Theodore Rubin, "The problem is not that there are problems. The problem is expecting otherwise and thinking that having problems is a problem."

What's so great about Agile is that it helps you focus the right amount of attention on each aspect of your organization, so it has the greatest opportunity to adapt and grow over time. This means your entire organization can adopt the stance of the restless expert rather than a complacent amateur— or disengaged dropout. This powerful adjustment can often make the difference between a lackluster organization and one that is vibrant, efficient, and full of life. And at the end of the day, isn't that the kind of organization we all want to build?

Agile Measurement
By Larry Maccherone

An Evolving Process

A flounder's environment is the ocean floor. His success as a fish depends only on feedback from above, so he has eyes only on the side that's looking up. Your organization once required a certain set of metrics because it lived in a certain type of environment. But the environment changed and your metrics likely stayed the same. It's time to evolve.

Early on, the movement between the various different stages of software's lifecycle was very expensive. Compilers ran for hours. Testing was labor intensive. Distribution of a completed product involved physical media and could take months to distribute. In this environment, it was critical to minimize the number of times you went through these costly transitions. Fittingly, the emphasis for feedback was on the process, with the goal of reducing rework over these expensive boundaries. Similarly, the success of a project minimally required that it be finished before funding ran out. So there was similar emphasis on the plan feedback.

However, the environment has changed. The costs of compilation, testing, and distribution have been driven close to zero. The biggest threat to success is not that you'll run out of money, but that you'll miss your market window. Rework is no longer verboten. In fact, it's much better to build something minimally usable and then rework it based upon usage feedback than it is to try to "build it right the first time." Like the flounder, which no longer needs feedback from below, we value feedback on the process or the plan less than we once did.

Our most valuable feedback is feedback on the product.

Early Agilists replaced these old metrics systems with qualitative insight, which works great on smaller teams. But Agile is going through another environmental shift. It's scaling up to larger projects and is starting to be used in environments that still have significant stage-gate transition costs (like hardware/firmware systems). In these environments, qualitative insight alone is insufficient. It must be complemented with the appropriate quantitative insight. So, the pendulum has swung and the value of appropriate measurement is clear, but we don't want to make the same mistakes that caused early Agilists to throw out the old measurement regimes.

In my years helping folks implement a metrics regime that balances *quantitative and qualitative* insight, while avoiding the pitfalls of pre-Agile metrics regimes, I've come up with the recommendations that follow.

1. Start with desired outcomes, not what's easy to measure.
Better measurement leads to better insights, which in turn leads to better decisions and eventually better outcomes. That's the chain of effect for measurement, so most people start by choosing measurements that are easy to acquire. However, measuring what's easy can drive the wrong behavior. Let's use a sports analogy to illustrate this point.

In 2010, Monta Ellis, with the Golden State Warriors, was the ninth-highest scorer in the NBA. Carmelo Anthony, with the Denver Nuggets, was the eighth-highest scorer. Measuring individual scoring totals is easy. You would assume that because they were prolific scorers, their teams would win.

However, the more they played, the less their teams won. Scoring is a function of two other measures: 1) the number of shots, and 2) the percentage of those shots that go in the basket. It turns out these two "stars" have low measures for No. 2, their shooting percentage. The only reason they are high scorers is because they take more shots. Now, if they were making more opportunities for shots, that might be okay, but that's not the case. Their team takes almost exactly the same number of shots per game no matter how much they play. They are literally stealing shots from their teammates who might have a better chance of scoring.

So, while the flow of learning goes from measures to outcomes, the way we should think about measurement should actually start with outcomes.

The NBA players should focus on the outcome of winning more games rather than being a high scorer. If they used the overall likelihood of the team scoring under various conditions as feedback, it would help them make better game-time decisions to achieve the ultimate outcome of winning. This brings us to our second and most critical distinction for Agile measurement.

2. Think of measurement as feedback, not levers.

So, if feedback emphasis is key to the success of Agile, the key to effective Agile measurement is to think of measurement in terms of feedback, not as the traditional lever to motivate behavior. This often devolves into keeping score, which is where the dark side of measurement starts.

There is a subtle, but important, distinction between "feedback" and "lever." Feedback is something you seek to improve your own perform- ance. Levers are used to influence others. The difference is more in how you use the measure than the measure itself.

For example, healthy use of a burndown chart tells the team members if they are on track with their commitment so they can make adjustments in time. The counterexample is a manager using burndown charts to red-flag projects in trouble. While it may drive improvement, nobody wants the red flag thrown at them, so the tendency is to keep the metric in the green re- gardless of the reality of the situation.

You can't make better-informed decisions if the metrics you are using to gain insight don't accurately represent reality. Rather, the manager could provide coaching on tools that the team members can use to improve their own performance—a subtle but critical difference.

3. Adopt a balanced measurement regime or none at all.

Balance in Agile measurement means having at least one measure from each of these areas:

- Do it fast
- Do it right
- Do it on time
- Keep doing it

Without balance of these four elements, it's easy to focus on just one. For example, if we focus only on "doing it faster," you will have a tendency to take shortcuts and not "do it right."

4. Use the Software Development Performance Index (SDPI) outcome measures.

1. Productivity (Do it fast)
2. Responsiveness (Do it fast)
3. Quality (Do it right)
4. Customer Satisfaction (Do it right)
5. Predictability (Do it on time)
6. Employee Engagement or Employee Satisfaction (Keep doing it)

These six outcomes are the elements of the Software Development Performance Index (SDPI), which is used to quantify insights about development work and provide feedback on how process and technology decisions impact the development team's performance. This fleshes out the four quadrants of balance provided in recommendation 3.

5. Balance qualitative and quantitative insight considering cost.

Sometimes it's too expensive or burdensome to get the exact metric that you want. Even when the actual cost is low, the perceived burden can be much greater, especially in an Agile environment. In some cases, the acquisition of developers is the limiting factor to your growth or even your minimal success. You do not want to burden developers unnecessarily. That means, in many cases you will have to live with qualitative insight.

Also, you want to frequently validate a hypothesis that you have (qualitative insight) by using metrics (quantitative insight). The results of that analysis will lead to more questions. Creating this virtuous cycle between hunches is very powerful and can lead to huge leaps forward in decision making. This requires support for ad hoc analysis. Rally connectors like the Excel plug-in, as well as APIs, data access toolkits, custom grids, custom reports, and custom dashboard panels, all help achieve this state.

Agile Metrics

In the move to Agile, overall goals are largely the same as before: to delight users with a quality product delivered in a predictable and efficient manner. Even after your Agile transformation, you will largely do the same "types" of things: analyze, design, code, test, release, maintain, and, yes, measure.

It's the perspective you take while doing these things that Agile helps improve.

The Importance of Vision and Culture
By Liz Andora

Helen Keller once said, "The most pathetic person in the world is someone who has sight, but has no vision." This isn't true for just individuals; it's true for organizations as well.

So how does your organization stack up? Does it have vision?

When people ask me to describe Rally and why it is such a special place, the first thing I share is how our vision and culture shape everything we do—an idea not only supported but also championed by our leadership. That is in stark contrast to many companies that are driven solely by technology, products, or profit. Together, our founder Ryan Martens and CEO Tim Miller guide us toward a single vision:

"At Rally, we believe empowered people who actually want to come to work are essential for solving today's big, complex problems. We inspire continuous innovation and collaboration in our customers; helping them empower their people to deliver a factor four increase in value to their businesses. We do this through our world-class software, coaching, and community services.

"We call it **RALLYING!**"

Ryan started this company in 2002 to solve not only the biggest software problems, but also the biggest world problems, and to empower citizen engineers. Tim joined Rally shortly thereafter to build a company as great as its people and where people enjoy coming to work every day. Ryan and Tim make a powerful combination, one that is rare, and share the belief that vision and culture are core to Agile environments.

Vision for the Future

The Rally vision has evolved over time. It was co-created by many employees—people from all levels of the organization—and is core to who we are. This shared visioning process is an important part of how Agile teams and organizations operate.

Our teams are self-organizing and have high accountability. Some reside within a functional area such as engineering, and some form and re-form cross-functionally depending on the demands of the business.

These teams are not necessarily sanctioned or driven by senior leadership. When employees at any level see problems or opportunities within the organization, they are encouraged to demonstrate leadership by forming a team to take action. For this to happen, employees require a clear understanding of where we are headed. In an environment with shared vision, employees are able to prioritize work and connect their work to the forward direction of the company. Without a shared vision it would be difficult for an organization to create high-performing, self-organizing teams.

Culture Counts

The next key ingredient to our success is our culture, which is shaped by these key values: Create Your Own Reality, Live Agile, Cultivate Trust and Respect, and Balance Our Lives.

The shaping of our values is a good example of the power of shared vision. We do this by running a process to create our True North. The True North expresses business needs that must be achieved in a certain time period, usually more than a year, and exerts a magnetic pull. Once this has been identified, a group of self-organized employees consolidates the data and drafts our values. When agreed to by a broad group of employees, the team develops a robust communications plan.

In addition to weaving the values into our daily living, each month we choose one value to spotlight. Employees share personal stories about how this value shapes their lives and impacts their work and interactions; they also recognize colleagues who they believe are true embodiments of it.

Next, the team creates videos that capture employees talking candidly about how this value affects our culture. They are viewed both internally and externally, and ensure that our values are not limited to our headquarters in Boulder, Colorado. It's important to us that these values get woven into other programs such as peer 360 evaluations, leadership development assessment and training.

To learn more about the True North process, refer to Pascal Dennis's book *Getting the Right Things Done*.

Values and Vision

Combined, our values and our vision create a wonderfully rich culture. We often hear from customers and partners that they know a Rally employee when they see one—proof that our work doesn't only show up in the office, but with our customers and partners as well.

As Simon Sinek observes in *Start with Why*, people are inspired not by the "what" and the "how" but the "why." "If you hire people just because they can do a job, they'll work for your money. But, if you hire people who believe what you believe, they'll work for you with blood, sweat, and tears."

Our culture is a key differentiator and performance driver. It gives us a competitive advantage in recruiting, retaining, and engaging people, driving innovation, enhancing productivity, and improving customer experiences.

At Rally we believe that we can help transform the way the world uses, consumes, and experiences software. We also can create citizen engineers who help others build successful businesses that have positive impact on customers, employees, the community, and the world.

Does your organization have a shared vision, one that inspires and rallies people to achieve greatness? Does that vision shape your culture? Do your leaders understand this dynamic and how it is core to your success?

As Antoine de Saint-Exupery says, "If you want them to build ships, make them yearn for the sea."

Agile Selling: Pulling Sales Forward
By Brendan Walsh

While most Agile literature focuses on product development organizations, Agile methods can also be hugely beneficial in running the sales side of an organization. As VP of International Strategy and Sales at Rally, my team and I approach almost everything we do with an Agile mindset.

Agile companies specialize in creating highly transparent cross-functional teams that partner closely with customers to solve complex problems. Through these teams, Agile companies focus on delivering the right things, instead of trying to deliver everything. Of course, this works only if we've created a truly cross-functional single organization.

The problem is that, because of some archaic precedent, salespeople are often left out of the product-development decision-making process entirely, which creates tensions between the two departments.

Product development typically accuses salespeople of making commitments to customers that the company is not prepared to deliver. Salespeople in turn believe product development can't get product out the door. Although they're in the same organization, these separate groups typically have two different cultures.

What's missing is a free-flowing stream of information that lays out what both teams can expect internally and, in turn, what our clients can expect.

Where Can You Begin?

From my personal experience, the best place to start this process is where education and communication intersect.

Before I began working in an Agile organization, the product delivery cadence I could tell my customers to expect was a bit nebulous. Typically the only way to get their voice in the room was through internal executive escalations. And only in escalation mode could I get product management onto calls or onsite visits.

When I joined Rally, I discovered the Scrum process for planning and guiding the direction of our products and witnessed how it created a very predictable delivery cadence that both my customers and I could rely on. We delivered new releases every eight weeks, and on top of that, I could attend our product development demo every two weeks to see the most up-to-date working code.

This regular cadence allowed me to do something I've never done before: with high confidence, I could sell into a roadmap that was well communicated internally and discuss product commitments with my prospects and customers 12 weeks in advance.

It was this level of predictability that helped me earn trust and allowed me to build out regional references about our ability to deliver—something I could never have done if sales weren't an integral part of the product delivery strategy.

Sharing the Path

Salespeople can both help and hinder the rhythm of an Agile enterprise. Most important, we teach customers about the unique value we deliver by working as a cross-functional organization and creating greater shared understanding of both internal and external expectations.

When we design our iterations or release commitments, we do so with the specific items our customers and business have signaled as most valuable. The beauty of this model is that we're deeply engaged in the expectation and commitment-setting process, so we're able to get more-transparent feedback. We also get to work within a more strategic system, which is made up of sales, marketing, and product development peers. This larger system becomes our company's Agile Value Stream.

Engaging and having a sense of worth and ownership in the Agile Value Stream has enabled me to build bridges with people I've never been able to in the past. This helps reduce the blame-game culture and increase our company's engagement of customers and flow of value to them.

One salesperson recently shared that he regularly educates his customers about how this process differentiates Rally from the competition. It's no surprise that his customers report that working with him resembles a true partnership, in contrast to their experience with software vendors who are good at "slinging software" but then forget about them.

One sales VP described how in his previous role it was common to have evaluations once every 6 to 12 months, each consisting of what-if scenarios with simulated data. By working in an Agile organization, the Agile Value Stream has allowed him to shorten those evaluation intervals to 1 to 2 months.

Agile businesses provide a level of transparency and interaction with their customers that really is unparalleled. As a sales professional I am confident that when you embrace this process as part of your value proposition, you will find a new level of trust and collaboration both internally and externally.

Agile Rollout Planning:
It's the Planning, Not the Plan

By Ronica Roth

Any Agile transformation begins with significant legwork—interviews, data reviews, research, and pilots—that helps determine if adopting Agile will bring the organization success. Once the case has been made, the next important task is to hold an Agile Rollout Planning session.

Like many Agile ceremonies, this workshop has a more meaningful purpose beyond just creating a deliverable; it's about helping the organization identify the whole picture, collaborate toward an outcome, and reach consensus on the path forward. What's more, it helps build cross-functional support—a key part of any Agile transformation.

Although we call it "rollout" planning, this principle can be helpful even if you're "already Agile" and just looking to take your organization to the next level.

Ideally, Agile Rollout Planning is a full-day meeting with broad representation. As with most critical collaborative meetings, having a facilitator is particularly helpful for keeping the meeting on track, capturing output and outcomes, and managing what can become heated conversations. A facilitator or other neutral attendee with Agile expertise and experience can also help minimize distracting arguments and allow the group to focus on mapping the future.

Success also requires an effective invite list, purpose, and agenda. While you want to tailor the agenda to fit your organization, a typical one may look something like this:

Purpose
To define an Agile rollout strategy and detailed plan that can be used for funding and executing the strategy, including outcomes and measures, process and practices, roles, and a timeline with review cadence.

Agenda
Notice that most of the agenda items are written as questions. The item has been addressed if the question has been answered to the group's satisfaction.

1. Executive briefing (particularly valuable if the executive sponsors can't be there the whole time).
2. What is Agile—its value and its models?
3. What are the specific goals and desired business outcomes of the transformation? How will we measure success?
4. What has already happened in our Agile journey, and what have we learned from that?
5. What are the roadmap milestones/events we need to consider for the transformation?
6. What are the value streams and/or groups that will adopt Agile? In what order will groups adopt Agile? How will we form Agile teams?
7. What tooling and coaching do we need to consider to support Agile adoption?
8. Based on our goals, what other items need to go on our organizational change backlog? (Consider: role changes, new metrics, changed artifacts, infrastructure, etc.)
9. Given all of that, what is our rollout timeline?
10. What risks and issues should we consider?
11. Who is on the Transformation Team that will lead and manage this adoption?
12. How will we manage escalations?

13. When will we hold check-ins/Retrospectives?
14. What is our communication plan?
15. Closing: Next Steps, Parking Lot, Action Plan

Invite List

Ideally, the purpose and agenda will indicate the invite list, which should include representatives from all the departments touched by the transformation. At the very least this includes IT/engineering groups like development and quality assurance, and most likely it will also include groups that represent the business, such as product management and/or business analysis.

You'll also need the participants to be senior enough to commit time, money, and people to the effort. They should be leaders who, once on board, can help guide others to see how the Agile transformation fits into the organization's plans for future success.

How to Launch a Team
By Tamara Nation

"How do you eat an elephant? One bite at a time."

That is the advice I always give to newly formed Agile teams. It's a reminder that all things, even great things, have a beginning. As you begin forming and launching a new Agile team, a great start can make the difference between success and failure.

Over the years, Rally has helped launch thousands of teams, and in this chapter we gather the collective wisdom of that experience to help you kick off your very first Agile team. As with any Agile endeavor, the first step is the co-creation of a thoughtful plan for success by the stakeholders and individuals. Our plan is created using a four-step approach that progresses like this: Lay the Groundwork; Build Your Team; Create Something Valuable; and Retrospect.

Lay the Groundwork
Before beginning your Agile transformation you must first ask two questions: What is Agile? and Why are we doing it? Everyone in the organization should answer these questions, from senior management to developers. This helps avoid a "checkbook mentality," or the belief that Agile is just for development.

Of course it isn't just about asking questions; you must make some initial decisions as well. The first big decision to make before launching your team is to define who will be on it and what they'll be working on.

Build Your Team

It is a basic human desire to be part of something bigger than ourselves. For most of us, our work lives create the biggest opportunity for us to do this in meaningful and impactful ways. In my experience, Agile teams are the best vehicles for unleashing the potential of your people and your company.

When searching for members for a new Agile team, look for those who already have good collaboration and communication skills. These individuals will thrive in the fast-paced and team-focused environment that Agile methods demand. For leaders of the new team, seek out personalities who can respect multiple points of view, articulate team challenges and opportunities, and help manage potential conflict either inside or outside the team. It takes time to create high-performing teams, so don't expect instant results.

Create Something Valuable

The value proposition of all Agile teams is their constantly improving ability to deliver tested, working code. This precious and highly valuable code delivery is defined by user stories, which are written to articulate the customer value of the software that is being built.

User stories provide the business direction and focus often missing from other software development approaches. Moreover, they provide the primary mechanism for the business to start and finish conversations about the product. User stories aren't meant to be thrown over a wall and coded, but to be part of a lively dialog between business experts and developers. This conversation helps ensure you are building the right thing.

Retrospect

Retrospectives are part of the foundation of a learning culture and among the most important aspects of any Agile transformation. Without taking time to stop, reflect, and make changes, we will never achieve the highly sought and amazing experience of a high-performance team. Many traditional project management techniques offer postmortems, but there is a critical problem with this approach. Postmortem literally means "after death." Do you really want to wait to uncover valuable insights until your project or product is dead?

Retrospectives in their simplest form consist of an all-hands team meeting, a facilitator, and responses to three simple questions: What went well? What didn't go as planned? What changes can we make to improve? It's key to really dig into those structural or personal issues that hold us back from doing our best work. Good Retrospectives are characterized by critical observations of the process, work product, or team dynamics.

The next step is to take these observations and insights and develop an action plan of small improvements for the next iteration or team cadence. Like user stories, small iterative improvements can drive the development of better teams and products.

"I was born with three teeth."
I like to start my time with a new Agile team by asking them to tell me something their colleagues don't know about them. The answers I hear are often amusing, sometimes revealing, and always help the team feel more at ease in the pressure cooker of a launch.

An Agile transformation can be challenging and requires a lot from the team. A great start helps facilitate the process and puts you and your company on a path to greatness. While these steps will help you launch teams, remember that each team, each iteration, and each day is an experiment. Approached properly, the process will enable participants to learn how to learn as an organization and your teams will get better and better over time. The team launch is just an initial step on the journey to greatness, and well begun is half done.

When Your Organization
Is Waterfall and You're Not

By Steve Lawrence

As a freshly minted ScrumMaster, I was given the responsibility of managing a project that would create a solution to move an existing mobile number to another telecommunications carrier for a major telco in New Zealand. At first I was worried about the deadline and wanted to offload the project, but I knew that would have caused another major project to fail. We needed to meet the government milestones and come up with a different approach.

Armed with this information, I proposed a Scrum-based delivery framework. While I endured many heated discussions with colleagues who suggested we follow a more traditional approach, by continually delivering and meeting each milestone, we convinced the naysayers to let us move forward.

The project delivered successfully within the mandated deadlines and created one of the most high-performing teams I've ever been a part of.

I learned a lot during this project, from negotiating and weaving my way through the indoctrinated templates and processes to negotiating small improvements for the betterment of the team. But the most important lesson I took away is that it's the small victories that count.

Pick Your Battles

Creating an environment where Agile people feel empowered is a difficult but essential part of the process. Early adopters must feel confident about the path they've chosen and understand the value they add.

There will be times when fledgling Agile teams in waterfall organizations must continue to provide the traditional status reports, Gantt charts and, yes, even the change-request admin rigmarole. In these situations it's important to pick and choose which battles you want to fight.

On one Agile project I worked, a senior manager insisted we maintain a Gantt chart throughout the entire process. During one of our regular status meetings, he got very upset when the Gantt chart showed we were tracking a week behind schedule. I explained we were up to date and that this was just a dependency on the Gantt chart that couldn't be closed until some future work had been completed. Although he wanted to escalate the issue to senior management, I suggested we wait until the end of the Sprint and, if we came in on time, discontinue the use of the Gantt chart altogether.

The team delivered as expected three days early and that was the last Gantt chart I had to maintain.

Toolbox

I believe that Agile is a toolbox filled with Concepts, Principles, and Practices. You don't need all of them to be Agile—you don't even need half. What's important is that you understand the concepts, practices, and techniques that add the most value to fledgling teams.

One of the most important tools, of course, is the team itself. Agile is a team sport, and like any good team sport, each player must work collaboratively to ensure the whole team is successful—not just that player's position. Therefore, it's important to always build the team culture and ethos.

The next important tool is transparency. I like to use visuals to track our progress and show our success. I have found these invite questions and help the team members feel proud of the work they're doing. What's more, it invites interaction and encourages other people and teams to take notice of our process. Slowly but surely they get drawn in.

Overcoming Challenges

In most traditional waterfall organizations, the powers that be want the certainty of fixed price, scope, and time. While I have no concerns with providing fixed price and timeframes, I always insist that scope have some variability. Otherwise we'd be setting ourselves up for failure from the start. This is an area where there is no negotiation. Small steps must start with this big one.

Another major hurdle are managers who feel the only way to do their job is by command and control. Unfortunately, these types of personalities thrive in waterfall organizations and somehow always find a way to become involved with our Agile journey. I have yet to uncover a surefire way to overcome these people, but I find that falling back on the guiding principle of "small steps" is the only way to remain on course and relatively sane. Even now, after coaching Agile teams for six years, I still find this one of the hardest challenges to overcome.

In waterfall environments it is important to create a solid foundation for our Agile house and then build slowly but surely from there.

It is a reality that in almost all major corporations, and some smaller enterprises, there will be an undercurrent of traditional waterfall thinking. But just like the old adage "Rome wasn't built in a day," one of the most important aspects of Agile is the process, the journey itself. The journey will be long and hard, but everything of value generally is. You'll soon discover that the lessons you learn along the way are as or more important than the projects you deliver.

Your Next Steps

By Bob Gower

The secret of getting ahead is getting started. The secret of getting started is breaking your complex overwhelming tasks into small manageable tasks, and then starting on the first one.

—Mark Twain

If this book has done its job, it's left you hopeful and with new ideas about how to improve your business life. This is a good thing. Agile is a path of action not scholarly contemplation. You realize the benefit only when you try new things.

This book will be useless unless you do something with it—and it's vital that you do. The complexity of our markets and technical environments is increasing daily. Not only are things changing rapidly, but the rate of change is increasing. This means that our businesses are sure to face more uncertainty in the coming years and we'll need flexible and Agile organizations to respond.

We know Agile is good for business, but we also believe it's good for people. Agile practices, with their emphasis on problem solving and efficiency, have the potential to help solve some of the toughest problems facing humanity. And we believe Agile is an important part of creating meaningful job opportunities for more people.

But where do we start transitioning? How do we eat this elephant? The answer is always: one bite at a time. This means we start with a vision—or perhaps only a hope—of what the world can be and only then find the next incremental step along that path.

Finding a vision you can believe in—and a next step you can accomplish toward it—is your first, immediate goal.

While Agile transformations often look overwhelming at first glance, all that's ever required of you is to determine the next step and focus on that step. If you're already on the path to Agile, this may mean expanding to other teams or improving your practices. If you're new to Agile, it likely means beginning to design your first team launch.

No matter your situation, you will need to get buy-in from others.

We've designed this book to help Agile champions achieve buy-in. We encourage you to share the information you find here with your teams and partners. Also visit our book's page (rallydev.com/agile-business-book/) and our company blogs (rallydev.com/community/) for more information and resources.

And of course if you're curious about getting help on your journey, we'd love to talk to you. Visit rallydev.com or email us at services@rallydev.com for information on our services and more.

Thank you for reading and best of luck on your journey.

The Story of the Book

This book has been some four years in the making. It's a book on collaboration and iterative development that was written collaboratively and iteratively. And part of iteration is failure followed by inspection and adaption. Here's the story of how this book came to be.

For Iteration One, I was overconfident and cocky and told my good friend Kevin that I could explain Agile to a business audience in eight pages. There are about six versions of *Agile in Eight Pages* on my hard drive, and though they forced me to think through many concepts—some of which became blog posts and talks—no version ever reached the level of simplicity and clarity I was looking for, and none were ever published.

Iteration Two came when I joined Rally Software and partnered with three other coaches, Steve Adolf, Isaac Montgomery, and Scott Dunn. We tried to set up weekly meetings—commitments that proved impossible for us all to keep given our frantic travel schedules—and even began an ambitious interview schedule. Our theory was that if we started collecting data, a pattern would naturally emerge and we'd shape it into a book.

At one point we petitioned the Rally leadership to give us a budget to come together to swarm on the book—we were sure we could finish it in a week if we just had time to focus. We were turned down, and rightfully so. Our plans were far too optimistic.

When Scott left Rally to focus more on his growing family and Steve left to finish his PhD, Isaac and I rebooted the project, complete with cost projection spreadsheets and an ambitious plan to co-locate and co-write. Turned down—sensibly—by Rally leadership yet again, Isaac admitted he'd lost steam and needed to focus his time on a new position he was creating for himself at Rally.

And here the project might have died if not for a few lucky breaks. I was reading Seth Godin's *Linchpin* when I realized that I had in my hands the perfect vision for a book on Agile: a loosely organized set of small pieces about the same topic that would each be able to stand on its own. Without the need for a single overarching narrative I was free to reach out for help from busy colleagues who could easily contribute. With help from Lara Vacante in Rally's marketing department, the other coaches and I spent a few months working on a random list of topics. About this time I realized that I was close but not close enough. We might get a bunch of content this way but we'd never have a real book.

It was at this point that Alex—my partner in love and life and herself an author of three books—turned to me and asked, "Do you have an outline?" and "Do you have an editor?" Without those pieces and a deadline, she assured me, we would never complete the project. And then she introduced me to her friend Michael Parrish DuDell—who as it turns out had worked with Seth Godin as managing editor of The Domino Project. Coincidence?

Michael and I worked together to flesh out a preliminary budget and plan—one that Rally accepted. And off we went. We developed an outline and iterated it several times based on feedback from colleagues within and outside of Rally. And these individual pieces were farmed out to 35 Rally employees to write.

As we progressed through the iterations, we even released a small increment of the book at the Agile 2012 conference. In the end, we developed a streamlined process that allowed for input from the stakeholders while also allowing for control and speed in the editorial process.

We used our own Rally tool to track progress so we could keep track of everything. Here's a screen shot of our task board:

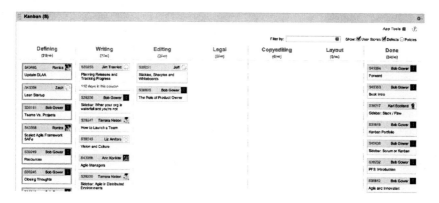

We also used Google Drive to manage the flow of documents and collaborate across time zones. We had authors from the United States, Australia, and Europe, editors in New York City, and stakeholders in Boulder, Colorado.

Eventually we iterated our way into a process that works. We're pleased with our process and hope you're pleased with the results.

The Agile Manifesto

agilemanifesto.org

We are uncovering better ways of developing software by doing it and helping others do it. Through this work we have come to value:

- **Individuals and interactions** over processes and tools
- **Working software** over comprehensive documentation
- **Customer collaboration** over contract negotiation
- **Responding to change** over following a plan

That is, while there is value in the items on the right, we value the items on the left more.

We follow these principles:

1. Our highest priority is to satisfy the customer through early and continuous delivery of valuable software.
2. Welcome changing requirements, even late in development. Agile processes harness change for the customer's competitive advantage.
3. Deliver working software frequently, from a couple of weeks to a couple of months, with a preference to the shorter timescale.
4. Business people and developers must work together daily throughout the project.

5. Build projects around motivated individuals. Give them the environment and support they need, and trust them to get the job done.

6. The most efficient and effective method of conveying information to and within a development team is face-to-face conversation.

7. Working software is the primary measure of progress.

8. Agile processes promote sustainable development. The sponsors, developers, and users should be able to maintain a constant pace indefinitely.

9. Continuous attention to technical excellence and good design enhances agility.

10. Simplicity—the art of maximizing the amount of work not done—is essential.

11. The best architectures, requirements, and designs emerge from self-organizing teams.

12. At regular intervals, the team reflects on how to become more effective, then tunes and adjusts its behavior accordingly.

The Author

Bob Gower

Bob Gower is passionate about innovative products and the people who make them. An author, speaker, and consultant, Bob has spent more than 15 years leading complex, creative projects across myriad sectors. Early in his career, Bob was the Director of Design and Production for the San Francisco Examiner and worked on the early digital presences of MSNBC, Elance, Newsweek, Discovery, and many other properties. After receiving his MBA from the Presidio Graduate School, Bob managed products for Silicon Valley startups, including MaestroConference and Genius Inc. He's currently an Agile Coach for Rally Software, where he specializes in enterprise-level Agile transformations. When not traveling, Bob lives in New York City. Get his latest articles at bobgower.com.

Contributors

Alex Pukinskis

Alex Pukinskis has helped dozens of software organizations transition to Agile development since giving XP a try in 2001. He has worked as an Agile coach through Rally and ThoughtWorks, and as an independent, helping organizations of all sizes succeed with Agile. Prior to coaching, Alex was developer and manager of software teams. Alex is a regular presenter at conferences, including Agile, Agile Roots, SD Best Practices, and Better Software. He is a Certified ScrumMaster Practitioner and holds a BA from the University of Connecticut. Alex currently works as a Lead Agilist for the Product Team at Rally, guiding the portfolio process and coaching the product group.

André Dhondt

For over a decade, André has led Agile adoptions, providing guidance to teams and organizations seeking shorter development cycles, higher quality, and more effective discovery of customer value. Playing various roles, from developer, manager, Product Owner, and ScrumMaster, he's done everything from hiring and building teams in startup environments to coaching teams for organizations with more than 100,00 employees. After receiving an MS in information science from Drexel University, André has continued his lifelong commitment to learning by organizing and facilitating discussions amongst local practitioners in Philadelphia, where he lives with his spouse and three children.

Ann Konkler

As an Agile Coach with Rally Software, Ann Konkler has worked with hundreds of individuals to help them hone the art of value delivery through Agile and Lean thinking. She especially derives satisfaction from helping others to understand and achieve the benefits of an adaptive work culture, fostered by collaborative leadership, motivated teams, and engaged people. Ann began her career almost 20 years ago as a computer programmer. Later roles included tech lead, business analyst, project manager, and then development manager for infrastructure, eCommerce, and PMO teams. Before coming to Rally, she was charged with leading Agile adoption in a Fortune 500 company for more than 1,000 people.

Ben Carey

Ben is an Agile Coach with Rally Software in Raleigh, North Carolina. His experience includes participating on Agile teams as a manager, architect, team lead, developer, tester, analyst, designer, and ScrumMaster. His passions are all grounded in helping teams find the essence of great software.

Brendan Walsh

As VP for Rally's International Strategy and Sales, Brendan is responsible for discovering new markets for Rally and launching Rally's business into those markets. He loves being in new regions of the world and measures his success by how passionate our new global employees, customers, and friends in the community become as they move closer to the Rally family.

Prior to Rally, Brendan was with IBM Software Group, Rational Software, and CCI/Triad in various lead sales and customer-facing roles. When he's not spending the night on airplanes, he prefers to spend his time with family and friends exploring Colorado and Utah on foot, bike, or skis.

Brent Barton

As former President of Agile Advantage—a product and services company, recently acquired by Rally Software, that helps organizations maximize the financial return of Agile software development projects—Brent has unique insights into the challenges from increased intensity that iterative and incremental development brings to the project portfolio. Brent graduated from San Jose State University with a degree in mathematics that has served well in development of AgileEVM, furthering the foundational research to meet business challenges in moving to Agile methods. Brent has an extensive background mentoring and guiding whole organizations toward Agility.

Charles Ferentchak

Charles likes nothing more than a Skunk Works project. At Rally his favorite projects involved creating prototypes to get fast customer feedback and quickly address customer needs. This passion led, in a logical transition, to his role in running Rally's customer hackathons. Coaching engineers to think audaciously and to trust their own abilities and talents over the common understanding is all part of a good day's work. In his free time, Charles loves to practice yoga and eat spicy food.

Chris Browne

Chris Browne is an Agile Coach and Application Developer with a passion for helping organizations learn how to innovate. A fan of hackathons, design thinking, and automated testing, Chris is able to leverage his experiences as a developer and test automation engineer to help teams improve their processes and supporting tools/infrastructure. Besides helping teams improve, he also develops custom extensions for the Rally application to help better integrate the tool with a customer's current environment and needs. A former triathlete and photographer, Chris now spends his free time producing music and DJ-ing.

Eric Willeke

Eric Willeke is a generalist software practitioner with more than 10 years of experience covering development, leadership, coaching, training, and consulting roles. Eric has continually demonstrated an ability to fit lean and Agile practices cleanly into organizations across an incredible variety of contexts, amplifying the chances of ongoing adoption.

Isaac Montgomery

Isaac is a Transformation Consultant and Agile Coach with Rally Software, where he pursues his passion for facilitating the organizational and cultural change inherent in achieving enterprise and business Agility in large, complex organizations. In his more than 20 years of experience holding management and consulting roles with organizations in the military, energy, financial services, and medical solutions industries, Isaac has learned that enabling meaningful and lasting change is ultimately about leadership—inspired, disciplined, inclusive, and committed leadership. In his free time you will find Isaac at the park with his twin sons or on the golf course destroying his self-esteem.

Jean Tabaka

As Agile Fellow in Rally's Office of the CTO, Jean continues a 30-year path of learning about principles, processes, and practices for people in software industries. She seeks a humane approach in bringing high value to communities of creators and consumers, and considers embracing disciplines beyond traditional Agile a delight: systems thinking, complexity theory, design thinking, and work in scaling empathy and vulnerability. Author of *Collaboration Explained* and a variety of other diverse Agile articles, Jean contributes to www.rallydev.com/agileblog and some 140-character assertions at @jeantabaka. When home in Boulder, Jean shares wine and gratitude watching a sunset over the Foothills.

Jeff Ellis

Jeff is a developer with Rally Software in Raleigh, North Carolina. He joined Rally in 2009 as part of the acquisition of Sixth Sense Analytics. Jeff became interested in Agile processes while working in the telecommunications industry, where releases could be years apart. He is passionate about building quality software and helping teams succeed. Outside of work, he enjoys golfing and camping.

Jessica Kahn

As a senior marketing manager at Rally, Jessica has extensive experience writing, branding, and producing campaigns that inspire people to embrace Agile and Rally. She is passionate about helping thought leaders appeal to specific audiences so they understand the message and take action. Before coming to Rally, Jessica held marketing and product management positions with ReadyTalk, Roxio (a division of Corel Corporation), and Novartis. She is a graduate of the Wharton School of the University of Pennsylvania, where she sang jazz a cappella. She thanks Rally for introducing her to Agile methods, which she uses extensively both at and outside of work.

Jim Tremlett

Jim Tremlett is an Agile coach at Rally Software with experience as a software product engineer, manager, and methodologist. With more than 20 years of experience in R&D laboratories, startups, and consulting organizations, Jim has come to appreciate the innovative buzz of product development. Jim particularly enjoys the challenges of coaching teams involved in large-scale Agile product development initiatives.

John Michael Martin

John likes gluing stuff together. Rally Software allows him to practice this passion in the role of coach, where he helps teams cohere and work together, and as a member of the platform extension services team, where he helps disparate software products interact and work together.

Julie Byrne

Julie is passionate about helping software development teams find the right tools for their projects. As a Technical Account Manager for the Pacific Northwest region at Rally Software, she has worked with many organizations to help them adopt the Rally platform for their Agile software development processes. Before transitioning to her current role, she worked at Rally as a Product Coach, guiding organizations through Rally platform implementations and integrations. Julie has also worked as a Product Owner and Product Manager. Outside of work, she enjoys running, hiking, and cooking.

Julie Chickering

Julie Chickering is an Agile Coach with Rally Software. She has coached many organizations, teams, and individuals as they transition to Agile, and has the proven ability to transfer job knowledge and skills to all levels. She is passionate about coaching people to a better and more fun work life. An internal coach at Travelocity before joining Rally as an Agile Coach in 2008, Julie brings more than 20 years of experience in the software development industry, in various roles. She lives in Dallas with her husband and teenage son.

Karl Scotland

Karl Scotland is a versatile software practitioner with over 15 years of experience covering development, project management, team leadership, coaching, and training. For more than 10 years he has been applying Lean and Agile methods, and most recently has been a pioneer in and advocate of Kanban. Karl is a founding member of the Lean Systems Society and the Limited WIP Society, a Coach with Rally Software in the UK, and is driven by helping organizations unleash the potential of their people to deliver a greater flow of value.

Ken Clyne

Ken is an Agile Coach with Rally Software, where he pursues his passion for coaching software development organizations of all sizes as they incre- mentally adopt Agile and Lean practices in order to build collaborative, continuously improving teams that deliver value early and often. Ken began his career more than 25 years ago developing compilers and air traffic con- trol systems. When he is not coaching you will find Ken outdoors golfing, kayaking, running marathons, or just messing around with his kids.

Larry Maccherone

Larry is moonlighting as Director of Analytics at Rally while he works on his PhD in software engineering (metrics) at Carnegie Mellon University ... or maybe it's the other way around. He believes that data visualization is like photography. Impact is a function of focus, illumination, and perspective. Larry is constantly creating new ways for Rally customers to leverage the data that they put into Rally as insights that will help them make better decisions and improve their performance. Prior to taking on his current position, he was an Agile coach for six years and prior to that was a serial entrepreneur, with his biggest success being a startup that he grew to $20 million in annual sales.

Laura Burke

As a Corporate Facilitator, Laura Burke owns the facilitation and cadence of Rally Software's planning. She is passionate about teams working together effectively, engaging on the topic by speaking at conferences, teaching Rally's *Scaling Collaboration* course, and training nonprofits. Laura is a graduate of the University of Kansas, where she studied conflict resolution, and is a proud Jayhawk. While not at work, she loves to hike and get lost while visiting new countries.

Liz Andora

As the VP of People at Rally, Liz has a strong background in leading human resources for large and small technology companies. She has a history of aligning people strategies with business imperatives, creating a diverse, engaging, and collaborative culture. Most recently, Liz was Vice President of Human Resources for Webroot Software, a provider of industry-leading security solutions. Prior to Webroot, Liz enjoyed a nine-year tenure with Sun Microsystems, holding various leadership positions, most recently the role of Director, HR Mergers & Acquisitions. Liz received her BA in political science and her MBA in marketing from the University of Colorado in Boulder. Liz's passion outside of work is spending time in the Colorado outdoors with her husband Chris and daughters Camille and Megan.

Mark Kilby

Since 1990, Mark Kilby has guided individuals, teams, and organizations to develop unique software and system solutions for government, industry, and academia. His roles have included software developer, technical lead, rocket scientist, principal investigator, technical architect, web development manager, methodologist, ScrumMaster, Product Owner, and Agile Coach (since 2003). His experience spans complete software development lifecycles for a variety of industries, including consumer services, publishing, telecommunications, security, finance, military, and space. He currently focuses on leadership development, growing effective distributed learning organizations, coaching coaches, and serving servant leaders.

Michael Ball-Marian

Michael is an internal Agile Coach with Rally Software in Boulder, where he coaches the product engineering teams. Michael has more than 15 years of experience in the software industry, including roles in support, operations, project, and product management, and as ScrumMaster. He is passionate about helping teams and organizations achieve flow, effectiveness, and "consistent awesomeness" (trademark pending). Michael enjoys spending time outdoors with his wife and daughter, as well as armchair philosophy, martial arts, and card game design.

Niki Kohari

Niki Kohari is an entrepreneur with a passion for people and products. Before her time at Rally Software, she was a PhD candidate in industrial/organizational psychology, studying topics such as employee selection, training, organizational change, and performance management. She also published in the areas of leadership, mental model development, and fairness in the workplace. Niki was one of the co-founders AgileZen and joined Rally after it acquired the company. She is now Director of Organizational Development and works on strategic initiatives related to employee engagement, leadership development, and scaling the awesome Rally culture!

Rachel Weston Rowell

Rachel is passionate about teaching and technology, and found the perfect mix of those as an Agile Coach at Rally. Her background in software development teams and as a manager of those teams and supporting organizations has helped foment a drive to connect smart people with great ideas so that they can continuously improve. When she is not coaching, facilitating, and learning, you can find her running around with her husband and daughter or in the kitchen masquerading as a novice chef.

Rick Simmons

Rick's Agile work began in the late '90s, with exposure to RUP and iterative approaches. His passion is focused around Agile/Lean concepts and flow-based work management in software development, infrastructure/operations and throughout the enterprise. Rick was a founding partner at Xteric Technology Group, a development and services firm in Cleveland, Ohio. From 2005 to 2010, Rick was at Constant Contact in Waltham, Massachusetts, where he held dual roles as Director of Agile Practices and Director of Web Services. He is a graduate of Case Western Reserve University, with a degree in computer engineering. Rick joined Rally as an Agile Coach in July 2010.

Ronica Roth

Ronica evangelizes all things collaborative, creative, Agile, and Lean with incomparable energy and passion. Her current mission, as Solutions Evangelist in Services, is to equip Rally to build learning organizations that honor the individual, give everyone the chance to do what they do best, and harness the power of teams to amplify great work and produce great stuff (including software). She also pursues Colorado's outdoors, skiing, language, travel, stories, and people.

Ryan Martens

Ryan Martens is the founder and Chief Technology Officer of Rally Software. Ryan founded Rally to make a major impact in the technology industry by moving it from a slow, wasteful product model to a fast, sustainable service model. Ryan's vision of a tech company with a social mission led to Rally being recognized with Good Co's Best For The World award, Rally's status as a certified B Corporation, and Ryan's talk at TEDx MileHigh, among others.

Ryan is a founding board member with Entrepreneurs Foundation of Colorado, a member of the engineering entrepreneurship efforts at the University of Colorado, and a mentor at the Unreasonable Institute and Boulder TechStars. In 2012, Ryan launched Rally For Impact, whose mission is to mobilize citizen engineers to solve the world's toughest problems.

Sean Heuer

Sean is an Agile Coach with Rally Software. He is a passionate and enthusiastic management consultant who has focused primarily on evangelizing Agile and Lean principles. He believes that we are defined not by the certifications we hold, but by the individuals and companies we are able to help. He believes in the power of people acting as a team and in organizations built to empower and elevate those teams. His competitive spirit gives him an unquenchable thirst for knowledge and an insatiable appetite for challenging work.

Stephanie Tanner

Stephanie is a Product Owner at Rally in Boulder, Colorado. She is passionate about user experience and loves to learn more about how customers are using Rally as an Agile tool. She started her career at Rally as a software engineer and quickly sought out a mentorship with the user experience team. Now, as a Product Owner, Stephanie hopes to continuously bring value to Rally's customers by delivering highly requested features. Stephanie enjoys many Colorado sports, including bouldering, skiing, and tubing. You may recognize her name from the popular '90s sitcom "Full House."

Steve Lawrence

With over 19 years in the IT sector as a manager, consultant, and coach, Steve has seen and experienced the good, the bad, and the ugly. Previously, he spent five years as a leading Agile Coach and practitioner to two of Australasia's largest Agile transformations (Suncorp and Telstra), as well as a large number of different organizations across Australia and New Zealand. Steve believes that Agile is a toolbox with a set of tools to be selected and adapted as necessary to deliver greater value to customers— value in terms of leadership and delivering successful outcomes. Steve is now the Lead Agile Coach for Rally Software across Asia Pacific.

Tamara Nation

Tamara Nation is a Coach at Rally Software, where she pursues her passion for enabling individuals to learn, grow, and thrive using Agile and Lean principles and processes. She has helped launch dozens of teams with their Agile and Rally tool adoptions and considers distributed teams to be her specialty. Tamara has spent 15 years working in a variety of roles on software development teams large and small. Other notable work experiences include being the solo production Oracle DBA for a team of 50, building a software support team from scratch, and leading web development teams for Fortune 100 companies. It was her experience as a technical project manager that led her to discover Scrum in 2008. Tamara is also student of linguistics, off-piste skiing, and meditation.

Todd Olson

Todd Olson brings technology thought-leadership and a pioneering, entrepreneurial spirit to aligning Rally's product strategy and execution efforts. Todd leads the evolution of Rally's proven Agile ALM platform for enabling software and product-driven enterprises to deliver 50 percent faster to market. Todd joined Rally when it acquired his company, 6th Sense Analytics, where he served as Chief Technology Officer and led the fundraising of $7 million in seed capital. Prior to founding 6th Sense Analytics, Todd was Chief Scientist of the Together business unit at Borland Software and the co-founder and Chief Technology Officer of Cerebellum Software, where he is the original inventor and creator of the Cerebellum data integration product. Todd began his career at MBNA as a database designer and software architect. He has a bachelor of science in electrical and computer engineering and computer science from Carnegie Mellon University and is a graduate of its Entrepreneurial Management program. Todd manages Rally's largest remote office, in Raleigh, North Carolina, where he lives with his family.

Zach Nies

Zach brings more than 25 years of engineering and product development experience to Rally as Chief Technologist. His whole career has been dedicated to bringing new products and services to market in startups and larger companies. One of his life core values is Learn, Do, Teach, Learn. This has led him to travel all over speaking publicly about how to create new business (he recently was among the speakers for the Lean Startup track at SXSW). He is a member of the Entrepreneurship Advisory Board for the University of Colorado's Silicon Flatirons Center and teaches technology entrepreneurship within CU's College of Engineering and Applied Science. He was a Mentor-in-Residence for the TechStars Boulder class of 2012.

References

Books

Adkins, Lyssa. *Coaching Agile Teams: A Companion for ScrumMasters, Agile Coaches, and Project Managers in Transition.* Addison-Wesley, 2010.

Anderson, David J. *Kanban: Successful Evolutionary Change for Your Technology Business.* Blue Hole Press, 2007.

Avery, Christopher M. *Teamwork Is an Individual Skill: Getting Your Work Done when Sharing Responsibility.* Berret-Koehler, 2001.

Blank, Steve. *The Startup Owner's Manual: The Step-by-Step Guide for Building a Great Company.* K & S Ranch, 2012.

Brown, Brené. *Daring Greatly: How the Courage to Be Vulnerable Transforms the Way We Live, Love, Parent, and Lead.* Gotham Books, 2012.

Cockburn, Alistair. *Agile Software Development: The Cooperative Game.* Addison-Wesley Professional, 2006.

Cohn, Mike. *Agile Estimating and Planning.* Prentice Hall, 2005.

Collins, Jim. *Good to Great: Why Some Companies Make the Leap ... and Others Don't.* NY: HarperCollins, 2001.

Covey, Stephen R. *The 7 Habits of Highly Effective People: Powerful Lessons in Personal Change.* Free Press, 1990.

Davies, Rachel, and Liz Sedley. *Agile Coaching.* Pragmatic Bookshelf, 2009.

Demarco, Tom, and Timothy Lister. *Peopleware: Productive Projects and Teams.* Dorset House, 1999.

Deming, W. Edwards. *The New Economics for Industry, Government, Education.* MIT Press, 2000.

Dennis, Pascal. *Getting the Right Things Done: A Leader's Guide to Planning and Execution.* The Lean Enterprise Institute, 2006.

Derby, Esther, and Diana Larsen. *Agile Retrospectives: Making Good Teams Great.* O'Reilly Media Inc., 2006.

Douglas, David, and Greg Papadopoulos. *Citizen Engineer: A Handbook for Socially Responsible Engineering.* Prentice Hall, 2009.

Eoyang, Glenda H., and Royce J. Holladay. *Adaptive Action: Leveraging Uncertainty in Your Organization.* Stanford University Press, 2013.

Gall, John, R.O. Blechman. *Systemantics: How Systems Work and Especially How They Fail.* Quadrangle, 1977.

Gilb, Tom. *Competitive Engineering: A Handbook for Systems Engineering, Requirements Engineering, and Software Engineering Using Planguage.* Butterworth-Heinemann, 2005.

Greenleaf, Robert K. *Servant Leadership: A Journey into the Nature of Legitimate Power and Greatness.* Paulist Press, (1977) 2002.

Greenleaf, Robert K. *The Servant as Leader.* The Robert K. Greenleaf Center, (1982) 2008.

Heath, Chip, and Dan Heath. *Switch: How to Change Things when Change Is Hard.* Broadway Books, 2010.

Kaner, Sam, et. al. *Facilitator's Guide to Participatory Decision Making.* John Wiley & Sons, 2007.

Kerth, Norman L. *Project Retrospectives: A Handbook for Team Reviews.* Dorset House Publishing, 2001.

Leffingwell, Dean. *Agile Software Requirements: Lean Requirements Practices for Teams, Programs, and Enterprise.* Addison-Wesley Professional, 2011.

Leffingwell, Dean. *Scaling Software Agility: Best Practices for Large Enterprises.* Addison–Wesley Professional, 2007.

Leighton, Ralph, ed. *Classic Feynman: All the Adventures of a Curious Character.* W. W. Norton & Co., 2005.

Lencioni, Patrick. *The Five Dysfunctions of a Team: A Leadership Fable.* Jossey-Bass, 2002.

Miller, Peter. *The Smart Swarm: How Understanding Flocks, Schools, and Colonies Can Make Us Better at Communicating, Decision Making, and Getting Things Done.* Avery Publishing Group, 2010.

Moore, Geoffrey A. *Escape Velocity: Free Your Company's Future from the Pull of the Past.* HarperCollins, 2011.

Moreland, Denise. *Management Culture: Innovative and Bold Strategies to Engage Employees.* Two Harbors Press, 2012.

Osterwalder, Alexander, and Yves Pigneur. *Business Model Generation: A Handbook for Visionaries, Game Changers, and Challengers.* John Wiley & Sons, 2009.

Patterson, Kerry, Joseph Grenny, Ron McMillan, and Al Switzier. *Crucial Conversations: Tools for Talks when Stakes Are High.* McGraw-Hill, 2002.

Pink, Daniel H. *Drive: The Surprising Truth about What Motivates Us.* Riverhead Books, 2009.

Reinersten, Donald G. *The Principles of Product Development Flow: Second Generation Lean Product Development.* Celeritas Publishing, 2009.

Ries, Eric. *The Lean Startup: How Today's Entrepreneurs Use Continuous Innovation to Create Radically Successful Businesses.* Crown Business, 2011.

Senge, Peter M. *The Fifth Discipline: The Art and Practice of the Learning Organization.* Doubleday, 1990.

Sinek, Simon. *Start with Why: How Great Leaders Inspire Everyone to Take Action*. NY: Penguin Group, 2009.

Tabaka, Jean. *Collaboration Explained: Facilitation Skills for Software Project Leaders*. Addison-Wesley, 2006.

Weinberg, Gerald M. *Quality Software Management: Systems Thinking*. Dorset House, 1991.

Wheatley, Margaret J. *So Far from Home: Lost and Found in Our Brave New World*. Berrett-Koehler, 2012.

Articles

Collins, Jim. 2009. "Level 5 Leadership: The Triumph of Humility and Fierce Resolve." *Harvard Business Review*. March 3.

Hoffstein, Brian. 2012. "The Exponential Rise of Lean Business." *Forbes*. July 5.

Marmer, Max, Bjoern Lassee Herrmann, Ron Berman, Ertan Dogrultan. "Startup Genome Report Extra: Premature Scaling." *Startup Genome*, Aug. 9, 2011, p. 10.

Miller, Mark K. "Peter Senge and the Learning Organization." *Encyclopedia of Informal Education*, 2001.

Patton, Jeff. "It's All in How You Slice It." *Better Software*, 2006.

Reynolds, Craig W. 1987. "Flocks, Herds, and Schools: A Distributed Behavioral Model." *Computer Graphics*. July: 25-34.

Smits, Hubert. "5 Levels of Agile Planning: From Enterprise Product Vision to Team Stand-up." Rally Software Development, 2006.

Warkentin, Merrill E., Lutfus Sayeed, Ross Hightower. "Virtual Teams versus Face-to-Face Teams: An Exploratory Study of a Web-based Conference System." *Decision Sciences* 28 (1997): 975-96.

Blogs

How to Staff Appropriately for a Successful Transition to Agile Product Management

http://www.rallydev.com/agileblog/2012/09/how-to-staff-appropriately-for-a-successful-transition-to-agile-product-management/

What Happens to Product Managers when Organizations Go Agile

http://www.rallydev.com/community/agile-blog/what-happens-product-managers-when-organizations-go-agile

What I Wish I Would Have Known when I Transitioned to Agile Product Management http://www.rallydev.com/community/agile-blog/what-i-wish-i-would-have-known-when-i-transitioned-agile-product-management

Video

Simon Sinek: *How Great Leaders Inspire Action*

http://blog.ted.com/2010/05/04/how_great_leade/

Bob Gower's Blog

bobgower.com

Rally Blog

rallydev.com/community

CPSIA information can be obtained at www.ICGtesting.com
Printed in the USA
BVOW03s1741280713

327184BV00001B/14/P

9 781939 337535